WEIRD ALBERTA PLACES

Humorous, Bizarre, Peculiar & Strange Locations & Attractions across the Province

Geraint Isitt

BLUE
BIKE
BOOKS

The Publisher: Blue Bike Books

Library and Archives Canada Cataloguing in Publication

Isitt, Geraint, 1971–
    Weird Alberta places : humorous, bizarre, peculiar & strange locations & attractions across the province / Geraint Isitt ; Graham Johnson, Roger Garcia, illustrators.

    ISBN-13: 978-1-897278-06-2
    ISBN-10: 1-897278-06-3

    1. Alberta—Miscellanea. 2. Alberta—Description and travel—Miscellanea. I. Johnson, Graham, 1975– II. Title.

FC3661.6.I84 2006   971.23   C2006-904128-8

Project Director: Nicholle Carrière
Project Editor: Rachelle Delaney
Illustrations: Graham Johnson, Roger Garcia
Cover Image: Roger Garcia

PC: P5

CONTENTS

INTRODUCTION 5

THE GREAT OUTDOORS.......................... 9
Animals at Their Best and Kookiest 10
One-of-a-Kind Landscapes 21

VERY SPOOKY, BUT NOT IF YOU'RE REALLY
TOUGH LIKE ME! 38
Ghost Towns.. 39
Ghosts and Creepy Crawlies 51
Mysterious and Historic 64

THE GREATEST EVER...AT LEAST SOMEWHERE 73
Best in the West 74
Canada's Best....................................... 79
Best in the World 89

LIKE LEGO AND TINKER TOYS, BUT MUCH
MORE IMPRESSIVE............................... 106
Bridging that Gap 107
Dam, That's Impressive...and Other Structures.............. 109
Malls, Museums and High-Rises: The Urban Jungle.......... 113

INTERESTING TRIVIA........................... 120
First in Class, or We're Just Better Than You................ 121
Wacky and Weird...Without the Padded Walls.............. 132
Old and Proud 144

MY COMMUNITY IS WEIRDER THAN YOURS!..... 152
Drumheller.. 153
St. Paul 157
Torrington... 161
Vulcan... 163

DEDICATION

A special thanks to Amanda for whom this book is written. Without your love, guidance, support and motivation, I would not be sitting here today. Thank you for providing inspiration, thank you for everything.

ACKNOWLEDGEMENTS

I would like to express my thanks to all at Blue Bike Books for giving me the opportunity to tell the world about Alberta. To Curtis Gillespie, Leslie Vermeer, Don McMann, Peter Roccia, Geo Takach, Lucille Mazo and my other instructors at MacEwan College who forced me to write and improve: I thank you for your guidance, dedication and love of the language.

To my classmates from my three wonderful years in the PROW program: many thanks for sharing ideas, words, experiences and laughter with me.

To my family, Mum, Dad, Susan, Barbara, Gary, Rick and Tara, Rhys and Carys: this book is for you guys to enjoy. I couldn't have succeeded without the support.

Thank you to Anthony, Leigh, Glenn, Christine, Dave, Shannon and others who recounted their travel stories to make sure I had not forgotten anything.

To the Wells and Oldenburg families: thank you for taking a writer into your hearts and homes and pushing me to this finished product.

INTRODUCTION

The word "weird" is perhaps the wrong word to be used in this book's title. Unfortunately, weird has a negative connotation that often offends people. I never objected to being called weird, and in fact, when I found out that I had been recommended to write a book tentatively titled *Weird Alberta Places,* I was quite pleased that I hadn't softened in my maturing years.

While the dictionary defines weird as "of a strikingly odd or unusual character; strange," many entries in this book fall under a much simpler category. Perhaps the word weird could mean unique, or interesting. Perhaps the word weird could mean odd and unusual. Whatever the meaning that is chosen, weird doesn't have to be bad. But, for the sake of argument, let's choose "unique" instead.

Why unique over weird? Firstly, weird always seems to bring up comparisons with Michael Jackson, and how many good things have you heard about him lately? On the other hand, unique offers a greater sense of pride. Unique conjures up a sense of originality and a sense of ownership that a person, community or even an entire province can be proud of. Unique, in its own way, is different.

Through my research and past exploration of Alberta, I have come across many interesting, odd, and unique sights that would easily fit within these pages. Very few of them would I call weird, in the highest order of the definition. Sure, a UFO landing pad may be a little strange, but is it altogether weird? I don't think so, but then again, I was recommended to write this book. That should tell you all you need to know about me.

Many of you who pick up this book will be looking for tales of the unknown, or perhaps just a good old-fashioned ghost story. You won't be entirely disappointed, but for the most part, I've steered clear of the ghosts and ghouls that haunt Alberta and only included some of my favourites. Ghosts and apparitions, while they are exciting, aren't necessarily weird or unique. Besides, Barbara Smith has written volumes on the hauntings around Alberta. So if you like ghost stories you should pick those up. You won't be disappointed.

The beauty of being me, or you for that matter, is that I have my own way of seeing things, as do you. The subjects and sites included in this book are ones that have caught my eye or left an impression on me. No two people will see things the same and I can only hope that others will read these words and see how unique, special, or just plain odd these places are. Or at least see why I feel they deserve mention.

Naturally, I probably missed some places or events that should be included. As I mentioned before, the sites and events included are ones that left a mark on me, and if I have missed something I truly apologize. Over the course of my researching and ultimately writing this book, I learned more about Alberta than I ever thought I would know.

Albertans should be proud of what we have to offer each other, other Canadians and the world when it comes to the unusual or impressive. Several of our communities can boast world-famous attractions, and others can boast about being the greatest in Canada or North America. Some, like Drumheller, need no introduction, and while Drumheller is not necessarily weird, its status on the world map as a leader in dinosaur fossil discovery is definitely unique and exceptional, and therefore included without hesitation.

Alberta also has its share of large, sometimes too large, roadside attractions. Some appear here strictly on the merits of their size, while others hold a special meaning to the town or community that they grace. A select few serve multiple purposes, and I'm sure you'll find them all interesting, wacky or just plain eyesores.

Not surprisingly, many of the unusual places in Alberta involve animals and nature. This book may leave you scratching your head with wonder at a heartwarming story about nocturnal salamanders, or questioning the safety of swimming thanks to a tale of a missing alligator in a central Alberta lake. Hopefully, the effects will stick with you for a long time.

And what about those man-made marvels that dot the landscape? Some have been mentioned, but only if they stand out in some way from the other concrete and twisted metal structures in the world. West Edmonton Mall is included; how could it not be when talking about the unique Alberta sites? Calgarians, don't worry, your city is well represented as well.

Some communities and events are included because they have one or two interesting and unique facts that separate them from anywhere else. It is amazing how many of Alberta's communities are Canadian or world leaders at something or other. It really is staggering.

The main purpose of this book is to show Alberta in its finest, funniest glory. A book of this nature must be written with a sense of humour and read with the need to chuckle. This book should be read as if you're a child on summer vacation, casting a spoon into a small lake or watching your dad chop logs for the fire as you tear into a bag of marshmallows. Most sites included should put a smile on your face and make you want to explore this great province. If tourism numbers go up next year, I'm asking the province for a piece of the pie. If tourism numbers decline, the weather will be at fault.

If you have any sense of adventure you'll want to see as much of this province as you can. Mingle with the locals, take the time to read the signs, and just look around with your eyes wide open and expectant. Whether you're looking for stuffed gophers, a giant pyrogy or the world's largest herd of free-roaming bison, Alberta has what you need. This province is yearning to be explored again and again.

Sit back and enjoy the book. You won't find any riddles or puzzles, but you will find that Alberta just might be the best place in the world to live. And again, if I have missed anything that should be included, I apologize. My intent was not to slight any of the wonderful opportunities Alberta presents.

Please take my personal tour of Alberta, stopping briefly at the sites that help define our section of the country. Laugh at the silly, shake your head at the strange and roll your eyes at the odd. Whatever your reaction, get out and visit. See for yourself just how good we have it and how uniquely we let the world know we have it.

My warmest and weirdest regards,

Geraint Isitt, May 2006

The Great Outdoors

Sometimes, just sometimes, animals and nature
leave an unmistakable imprint on a location, a town
or even an entire province. Such an area might be designated
an historical point of interest, a World Heritage Site
or simply the only region in Alberta that boasts
a type of tree, ecosystem or muskrat.

With a bounty of forests, deserts, lakes, rivers, streams
and mountain passes to inspire, impress and
foster the growth of animals and plants,
Alberta's landscape never disappoints.

The following entries are sure to capture the imagination,
leave you scratching your head or just plain laughing.

ANIMALS AT THEIR BEST AND KOOKIEST

ALBERTA BIRDS OF PREY CENTRE
COALDALE

Situated on 28 hectares of wetland, the Alberta Birds of Prey Centre is Canada's largest birds of prey facility. The centre, which guarantees an unbelievably wild experience, features hawks, eagles, falcons and owls of Alberta.

A drive to the centre, located near Coaldale in southern Alberta, is well worth the trip. The chance to see one of these birds in flight or up close is too good to pass up.

The centre seeks to conserve nature, and it follows several tricky but fundamental steps to ensure this mission is accomplished. First and foremost is the rehabilitation and releasing of injured birds into the wild. Step Two: captive breeding to increase endangered species levels. Step Three: the study of birds and their habitat, and Four: educating the public about the plights and wonders of Alberta's birds of prey.

For simply being a world-renowned and respected facility, the Alberta Birds of Prey Centre stands alone within Alberta and the world. And if you think this place is for the birds, you're right. But it's also for people to appreciate them.

And Speaking of Birds...

At the Ellis Bird Farm near Lacombe, visitors walking around a functioning farm will more than likely be impressed by the "world's largest collection of functional bluebird nestboxes."

During the open season, there is no admission charge, except for a scant $3 for a guided tour. Off-season activities include educational programs on cavity-nesting birds, winter bird feeding and backyard habitat.

THE ALIX ALLIGATOR

ALIX

It all started in 1979, when a resident of Alix, Alberta, witnessed a dark object moving across Alix Lake. Since that time, many other people have reported seeing the mysterious creature living in the lake's calm waters. Affectionately named "Alix" after the town, the creature gives this small central Alberta town its own Loch Ness Monster.

Many locals speculate that "Alix" might be an alligator that was released into the lake when it grew too large for its owners to manage. The possibility that it may be a sturgeon, a prehistoric fish still swimming in several Alberta rivers, has been thrown about as well. The sturgeon theory sits best with biologists because sturgeons grow throughout their entire lives, and the bumpy ridges along their backs make them look rather reptilian.

Between 2001 and 2002, there were four reported sightings of Alberta's most notorious lake visitor. To date, Alix has been content to feed on fish and plant life in the lake, and has kept out of trouble with the locals.

Bill Cogginns, a wildlife biologist, reckons that the warm spring-fed water may be providing the alligator (if it is indeed an alligator) with an unusual micro-environment that keeps him fed and healthy for the summer months. But while Alix is very active during the summer, how he survives the less-than-balmy weather that alligators are used to down near the equator has some people puzzled.

But is Alix an alligator? As with Scotland's mysterious monster, photo evidence surrounding the creature is questionable. Dark objects have been photographed on the surface of the water, but they are too blurry to identify.

Alix can be seen frequently throughout the year at various parades, events and gatherings. The town has adopted the alligator as its mascot, and he hates being mistaken for a crocodile.

APPALOOSA HORSE CLUB OF CANADA
CLARESHOLM

Follow the Queen Elizabeth II Highway south of Calgary and you will pass Claresholm, home of the Appaloosa Horse Club of Canada (ApHCC). The Appaloosa, or "spotted horse," is one of the oldest recognizable breeds of horses and existed long before recorded history. What makes Claresholm so special is that it is also home to the Appaloosa Museum.

The aim of the museum is to collect, preserve, record and display artifacts, relics, books, pamphlets, publications, papers, documents, photographs and other materials illustrative of or of interest to the history of the Appaloosa breed of horse. Currently, the museum is trying to establish a Hall of Fame for the horse and the people who have contributed to the breed.

Perhaps not weird in the truest sense, but such one-of-a-kind sites help set Alberta apart. Besides, Appaloosa is way cooler name than Hanoverian.

ELK ISLAND NATIONAL PARK

Oh give me a home, where the buffalo roam, with deer, elk and moose side by side. That home would be Elk Island National Park, the only park in Alberta where the aforementioned critters roam together freely.

Birdwatchers shouldn't feel left out either, for the park has over 230 species to spot and offers "birdies" of another kind with a nine-hole golf course as well. With over 90 kilometres of trails and several lakes providing canoeists ample opportunities for short trips, the park is a great place to spend the day, just roaming around. Canada's first federal wildlife sanctuary offers you the best chance of seeing wildlife if you're roaming at dusk or dawn.

Another first for Canada located in Alberta—does this province rock or what?

And Speaking of Buffalo…

A wonderful Alberta holiday can be had by taking the "Trail of the Buffalo," an exciting and informative trip around east-central Alberta. When outlined on a map of Alberta, the Trail actually forms the shape of a buffalo, complete with horns. The Trail offers 75 sites, some in cities and towns, others in rural locations, which will appeal to all. Step back in time, learn a little history and soak up Alberta at its purest. Just watch out for the buffalo; sometimes they actually charge cars.

BIG
GARGANTUAN &
RIDICULOUSLY
OVERSIZED

Aaron the Blue Heron

Situated north of Edmonton, Barrhead is nestled in green parkland and home to a variety of bird and animal life. A popular spot for animal gazing and birding, the area offers the chance to see many types of fowl. Plus, it provides the town a chance to celebrate one of the prettiest birds in the region. While most people have seen ducks and geese, fewer have had the chance to see herons, specifically the blue herons that reside in many of the lakes around Barrhead. For this reason, the town had Trygve Seland, builder of many of Alberta's monuments, construct Aaron the Blue Heron in 1984.

Built of wire mesh, rebar and concrete, Aaron stands 2.4 metres tall with a 1.2-metre-high pedestal, giving him an impressive 3.6-metre height. With his long, curved neck and his powerful wings tucked firmly at his side, Aaron stands tall and proud for locals and visitors to see on the corner of 49th and 50th Streets. Highly visible and easy on the eyes, Aaron is a beautiful specimen of a beautiful species.

"HONEY CAPITAL OF CANADA"
FALHER

Known as the "Honey Capital of Canada," this town made the list in 2006 as a judge's choice in the Hockeyville contest sponsored by the CBC. The contest, which was limited to 50 communities selected from across Canada, was a big success. The Falher Wannabees finished as the top Hockeyville team in the Northern region, but lost out on the chance to host an NHL exhibition hockey game in their own arena by not winning the overall prize. Honeybees and hockey go hand in hand, so it was a natural choice…I guess.

Back to business, and business is sweet. Falher and the surrounding area produce 10 million pounds of honey a year with some 45,000 beehives. This volume represents 40 percent of all honey produced in Canada. No wonder the nickname for the region has stuck—no pun intended.

With such an emphasis on honey, it is no wonder that Falher is also home to the largest bee. The bee was built in 1990 to coincide with Falher's first Honey Festival. It measures nearly 7 metres long and 2.4 metres wide. Naturally, a bee this big would need a big hive as well, and Falher has the world's largest beehive—built as a three-storey playground slide that overlooks the town. And for the people who find giant bees and beehives not quite fun enough, there is always the chance, like at every bee festival it would seem, to see someone wear a beard of bees. I think I'll stick to posing for a picture under the giant bee.

TRUMPETER SWANS
GRANDE PRAIRIE

Ducks are common, geese can be seen everywhere (especially near golf course water hazards, where I tend to spend most of my golfing time), but the trumpeter swan, the rarest of all swans in the province, is a little less visible. Unless of course you travel to Grande Prairie, where over two-thirds of Alberta's trumpeter swans flock.

In a 2000 survey, 608 trumpeter swans were counted in the Grande Prairie area, up from 72 in 1957. Not only are the trumpeter swans the rarest of swans, they are also the world's largest waterfowl, and pairs mate for life. With 404 adult swans counted, the odds of the population growing are good.

The trumpeter swans are so important and revered in Grande Prairie that the city emblem incorporates them, and the city's mascot is…yup, a trumpeter swan. Don't know whether or not the city will change its name to Swan Lake, though.

FRANCIS THE PIG
RED DEER

Remember the charming movie *Babe: Pig in the City*? Well, citizens of Red Deer had their own pig in the city. Affectionately named Francis, this pig wandered the parklands of Red Deer for five months back in 1990.

After escaping from a local abattoir, Francis found refuge in the lush parklands scattered throughout Red Deer. Hog production and processing is an important staple of Red Deer's economy, but Francis wanted a little more than what was allotted to him. By the time this freedom-loving pig was caught, he had become so loved by the city that he was allowed to live out his remaining days on a local farm. Francis—or rather, Francis' statue—now resides in a local park as part of the Ghosts of Red Deer, a walking tour that visits six statues in the downtown core. Francis went from slaughterhouse to penthouse; talk about living high on the hog.

LONG-TOED SALAMANDERS
WATERTON LAKES NATIONAL PARK

Curse humans and their need to doze, pave and build roads so they can access places of beauty and wonder. Did anyone stop and think how modifying the road that runs by the information centre in WLNP would affect the poor little long-toed salamander? Obviously not. The salamander was made to suffer, but humans proved their worth and came to the rescue.

It isn't entirely our fault. Salamanders are small in size (10 to 17 centimetres long), and they are nocturnal and burrowing animals; as such, it can come as a surprise when they are detected. Trying to get an accurate count on their numbers can prove extremely difficult. Such was the case in Waterton, until road improvements unearthed a salamander population.

In the fall of 1991, a park employee noticed the salamanders struggling to climb the new curbs on the road that bisected their migratory path to Linnett Lake. The curbs were so steep that it took the salamanders a long time to climb them, if they could at all. This led to a large congregation of the animals on the road—a very dangerous spot for little salamanders.

Community volunteers came to the rescue for about a week in April 1992. On cold rainy nights, these volunteers manually lifted over 2000 salamanders off the road and over the curbs so the little guys could continue on their migratory path. I'm sure the salamanders thanked them in a way only salamanders could. This discovery led to monitoring and testing of alternative ways to help the salamanders, and eventually, rough, sloping "salamander-friendly" curbs replaced the old ones and modifications were made to water drainage. And the salamanders lived happily ever after, aside from being called newts.

WHOOPING CRANE
WOOD BUFFALO NATIONAL PARK

A haven for the largest herd of free-roaming buffalo in the world, Wood Buffalo National Park has also played a vital role in protecting the most famous endangered bird in North America—the whooping crane.

The whooping crane is the tallest bird in North America, and it uses an unusual flying technique of spiraling and gliding, which enables it to save energy and cover long distances. Flights as long as 10 hours covering 750 kilometres are not uncommon, which is good because the bird flies over 4000 kilometres from Texas, where it winters, to northern Alberta, where it nests. In flight, the bird holds its neck straight out in front of it and its legs stretch out behind it, giving it a very unique silhouette.

Back in 1941, it was believed that only 22 wild whooping cranes existed. By 1993, 150 birds had been born to 16 descendants of that original group. Wood Buffalo is Canada's largest and one of the world's largest national parks. In terms of area it is larger than Switzerland.

And Speaking of Birds...

Edmonton also offers its people another large structure. When Pope John Paul II visited Edmonton in 1984, a Peace Dove was created to honour his appearance. Originally built near Namao on a farmer's field as an outdoor religious cathedral, the Catholic School's society moved it in 1988 to a hill overlooking the River Valley. With a wingspan of 17 metres, it truly is amazing.

ONE-OF-A-KIND LANDSCAPES

BADLANDS
DRUMHELLER

Alberta's badlands contain all of Dinosaur Provincial Park and are a sight to behold. Whether you are staring at the hoodoos or cavernous gullies carved into the sandstone, the badlands are a natural marvel full of ancient surprises and promises for the future, even the short-term future.

Once, long ago, the area was a lush wetland so great that even the dinosaurs could survive there, but that era brought forth the snow-capped glacial ice age, which in turn led to what can only be described as the arid, desert-like landscape that remains. Plants and wildlife have adapted to the new conditions and will continue to.

In an isolated spot of the badlands lies Horseshoe Canyon, a region with three different ecosystems: prairies, woodland slopes and badlands. Prairie grasses are found here, once food for the buffalo that roamed the region. Shaded areas house white spruce, wild roses and other bushes, offering shelter and protection from the sun that burns the coulee walls.

The dinosaurs in Drumheller get most of the attention, but the badlands will keep you interested and intrigued, and make you feel a little small.

Crows and Nest

Have you ever been out and about and thought that the birds were watching you? Well, if you travel to Blairmore in the Crowsnest Pass, your fears will be realized. Perched high atop a telephone pole are two crows, looking east and west along the Crowsnest Highway. Their bright yellow eyes seem to follow your vehicle for miles, and on more then one occasion they've made me and my passengers look up at the sky, expecting something from an Alfred Hitchcock movie.

A little larger than normal crows (although I have seen some ravens in Banff National Park that rivaled the size of chickens, so maybe other birds are just bigger in Alberta), these feathered omens of bad tidings do nothing but confirm to tourists that crows are indeed found in the Crowsnest Pass.

BANFF PAINT POTS
BANFF

This site is very popular with hikers, skiers and snowshoers alike. It is made up of three circular ponds that are so unique, even Mother Nature herself marvels at them. Each of the ponds is fed by oxide-bearing springs, but each pond has a distinct colour: red, orange and mustard-yellow.

Perhaps it was the work of animal spirits that stained the pools, but the highly spiritual Native people collected ochre from around the pools and combined them with animal fat or fish oil to make paint, which was used for body or rock art. The ochre was also used in many ceremonial rituals.

Not to be outdone, the Europeans, seeing the opportunity to add to the welfare of Canada's economy, began mining the ochre in the early 1900s and shipped it to paint factories in Calgary.

BODO ARCHEOLOGICAL SITES
PROVOST

Located just south of Provost, this archeological area is made up of the Bodo Bison Skull and Bodo Overlook sites, which have revealed artifacts from aboriginal encampments dating back to 3000 to 5000 years ago, as well as some younger finds, from 500 years ago.

Still in its infancy as a site, it was discovered by oil and pipeline workers in 1995. The community is hoping to open an interpretive centre, offer a public archeological program and have walking trails. A significant number of arrowheads, buffalo bone fragments and remnants of pottery have been found in the area, and such finds should lead to greater public interest.

NEUTRAL HILLS
CONSORT

Besides being the hometown of k.d. lang, Consort is also located near an area known as the Neutral Hills. Twenty-four kilometres north of town, these colourful hills have a history that must be shared. Their name came about when the Plains People set the area aside as a hunting preserve, where no fighting or marauding could take place.

According to the legend, the Great Spirit had a hand in raising the land to form the hills so the two warring tribes could not come together. The Plains scouts could hardly believe when the hills just sprang up in front of them. The hills provided a surplus of food, berries and water for both tribes. The scouts made peace at Little Gap after a great council.

It's just a pity that the same thing can't be done around the world today.

CONTINENTAL DIVIDE

Serving as Alberta's only natural border, the Continental Divide runs from Alaska to Mexico, and it offers some of the most spectacular scenery in the Alberta's Rocky Mountains.

The Continental Divide is an interesting and wonderful phenomenon. Many streams and rivers flow from the glaciers that cap the highest peaks of the mountains. Water leaving the peaks of the Continental Divide flow either two ways: east or west. The water leaking into Alberta continues east until it reaches the Hudson Bay, or some point in between, while the west-flowing water eventually runs to the Pacific Ocean.

Many hikers flock to locations within Banff, Jasper and Waterton National Parks, and the regions nearby to tackle the treacherous trails leading to the pinnacles that set the water is motion, so to speak. The hikes may be hard and dangerous, but the views from the top are well worth the risk.

WRITING-ON-STONE PROVINCIAL PARK
COUTTS

Not content with simply being on the Alberta-Montana border, the Coutts region offers up some of Alberta's best and most unique attractions. The region is home to some very impressive natural wonders. Writing-on-Stone Provincial Park contains the largest concentration of rock art, created by Plains People, on the Great Plains in North America. In 1977, a portion of the park was made an archeological preserve, to protect the over 50 rock art sites with thousands of figures.

Unfortunately, the rock art has continued in more recent years, as graffiti artists have found time and space on the rocks of the park. But there is hope that the damage will stop. Since the park is now an archeological preserve, the fines for vandalism or damaging any natural objects within the park can be as high as $50,000, a total that would stop me from pretending I had artistic talent.

The beginnings of Writing-on-Stone Provincial Park go as far back as millions of years. When the glaciers started receding some 12,000 years ago, the immense volume of water carved through the sandstone and created the valley in which the Milk River now flows, presenting the area with some phenomenal natural attributes.

No visit to the park is complete without stopping to see the Hoodoos, giant mushroom-capped formations of sandstone. They get their shape from years of frost and driving rain, which eroded the softer sand under the harder rock layers that now form the cap.

The site also has a recreated North-West Mounted Police Post located on its original site. As far as archeological sites go, few are better throughout the world. But tell me this: if a picture is worth a thousand words, how many words are thousands of images worth?

FRANK SLIDE
CROWSNEST PASS REGION

This region is world renowned, one of the most beautiful and unique places on earth, and right in our own backyard. Perhaps the most famous of the Crowsnest Pass' attractions is the town of Frank and the Frank Slide. On April 29, 1903, at 4:10 AM, nearly 82 million tonnes of limestone came crashing down Turtle Mountain and took part of the town of Frank with it. The slide was over in about 100 seconds, but it left a kilometre-wide path of destruction, with 100 people in it. Seventeen miners were trapped inside the mine, but they miraculously dug themselves free. Only 23 townsfolk managed to survive the slide, and only 12 of the 70 or so bodies that were buried under the carpet of rocks were found.

Today, a memorial grave stands at the west end of the road through the Frank Slide area, and a little further west, building foundations of the former town and a lone rusted fire hydrant are visible. After the slide, the mine reopened and stayed open until 1917, and the town gradually moved north to its present location. Around 6000 people call Frank home today, proving that man can triumph over nature.

The Frank Slide is a landscape feature of unique geologic and historic interest. It is known to earth scientists around the world. Three generations of geology students have read and studied pictures of the slide, and many of them have visited the site.

And Speaking of Mines…

Also in the Crowsnest Pass region is the site of the Hillcrest Mine, home to Canada's worst mining disaster. On June 19, 1914, 237 men began their 1.6-kilometre-long hike up the path to the entrance of the mine. At 9:30 AM, thunderous explosions ripped through the mountain. Sadly, 189 men died that day, and only 46 men were rescued.

The cause of the blast is unknown; perhaps a slide triggered sparks that ignited methane gas. Visitors can see three mass gravesites and other grave markers at the Hillcrest Cemetery, commemorating and honouring the dead from the 1914 disaster.

GOOSE MOUNTAIN ECOLOGICAL RESERVE
SWAN HILLS

In an area known for its grizzly bears, this unique section of land in Swan Hills has been set aside for hikers, photographers and lovers of nature—but only those on foot.

This unique area is home to 16 plants that are rarely found Alberta, including orchids. The high elevation of Swan Hills, 1180 metres above sea level, plays a part in producing this sub-alpine ecosystem not found anywhere else in the province.

Next time you're in the area, plan a trip to see the flowers. Stop and smell them if you like, just don't pick them. And please, keep off the grass.

DINOSAUR TRACKS
GRANDE CACHE

Dinosaurs are not just limited to Drumheller; up in Grande Cache you'll actually be surrounded by one of the world's best dinosaur track sites. Now, that doesn't mean you'll see an oval track where dinosaurs used to run the 100, 200 or 800 metres. The tracks you'll see have been preserved on the rocks at the Smoky River Coal Ltd. site. With 12 tracks over a 25 km^2 area, it simply is a must-see destination, and one that stands among the best in the world.

And Speaking of Dinosaurs...

A young local girl named Wendy Sloboda stumbled upon a major discovery back in 1987 in Warner, Alberta. After finding what she believed to be an egg, she sent it off to a professor at the University of Calgary who in turn sent it to a professor working at the Royal Tyrrell Museum of Paleontology. Wendy's find turned out to be a piece of a dinosaur eggshell. A crew was immediately dispatched to the area, hoping for a site similar to the one in northern Montana that had yielded dinosaur eggs and remains.

After days of searching turned up little, paleontologist Kevin Aulenback, while sitting down for a bite to eat, saw a piece of eggshell on his right, and to his left a piece of embryonic femur. A crew came out a few days later and uncovered a huge find: an 80-percent-complete nesting site of hadrosaur (duckbill) dinosaurs.

HEAD-SMASHED-IN BUFFALO JUMP
FORT MACLEOD

In southern Alberta, not far from Fort Macleod, the province has something in common with Machu Picchu, the Taj Mahal and the Egyptian pyramids. In our backyard, we have a World Heritage Site. Pretty impressive, huh? The aforementioned locations are revered the world over; perhaps it's time for Albertans to boast about their buffalo jump.

With a history stretching back nearly 6000 years, the buffalo jump has remained virtually untouched, offering a glimpse into ancient ways and how things evolved over the years.

Strategically located opposite the prevailing winds so the buffalo couldn't smell the kill zone, the buffalo jump allowed aboriginal people to drive thousands of bison to their deaths over the years.

The remnants found at the bottom of the cliff tell of advancements in tools and techniques that helped the Plains People adapt over time.

The 10-metre-deep bone deposits testify to the success of the hunts. The stratified deposits preserve the kills and show an evolution in the tools used to skin the carcasses and carve the meat.

This unique piece of land tells us more about our history than most other heritage sites in Alberta. Why we fail to celebrate such an amazing location is beyond me. And as for the buffalo, unlike the lemmings, at least they were corralled and chased over a cliff.

Rainbow Trout

The Alberta angling record for rainbow trout is somewhere around 9 kilograms; the fish was caught in Maligne Lake in Jasper National Park. The rainbow trout that stands behind the first exit past the McCains Processing Plant in Chin is slightly less than 5 metres long. This fish would totally shatter that record.

Chin, conveniently located on Highway 3 near Taber, is home to the Chin Coulee Trout Farm, and its rainbow trout monument was constructed as a promotional symbol for the farm. Unfortunately, the front side fins are missing, which leads me to believe that this fish likes the rough stuff and would put up a big fight when hooked.

Any way you look at it, this rainbow trout would make for a big pan fry around the campfire.

HERITAGE TREE FOUNDATION

Originally an Ontario program created to locate and celebrate historic trees, the Heritage Tree Foundation branched out in 2002 to include the Alberta Heritage Tree Project. To qualify as a heritage tree, a tree must be interesting by virtue of age, size, shape, special interest and/or location and history. These may include individual trees, avenues, groves, shelterbelts, tree gardens, arboreta and sites of botanical or ecological interest.

With a book illustrating Alberta's Heritage Trees due out in 2007, Alberta communities have until October 31, 2006, to nominate a tree that meets the Foundation requirements.

Unfortunately for me, the ficus I managed to keep alive for five years doesn't count for the project. The tree I used to climb in my backyard just might, though.

KALYNA COUNTRY ECOMUSEUM
KALYNA COUNTRY

What exactly is an ecomuseum and what is so special about the Kalyna Country Ecomuseum? Both are very good questions with very good answers. Firstly, an ecomuseum in the general sense is an expanse of land that includes many cultural and historical sites. The Kalyna Country Ecomuseum happens to be the largest ecomuseum in the world, covering over 20,000 km².

Kalyna is the Ukrainian word for the highbush-cranberry plant commonly found in this area, between Edmonton and the Saskatchewan border. In fact, the Kalyna berries were an important food source for the pioneers, settlers and Natives of the area.

Located within the ecomuseum is a portion of the Victoria Trail, the oldest road in Alberta, which leads to both the Victoria Settlement and the Métis Crossing, a region recently created to celebrate Canada's Métis people. Most of the early trailblazers in the West passed through the region, and there are monuments to honour them in various Kalyna communities.

In the late 1800s, the Kalyna region attracted an influx of settlers, many of whom were Eastern European, and thus it became the oldest and largest agricultural community established by early Ukrainian pioneers.

This legacy is evident in the more than 100 Byzantine Rite churches that dot the landscape of this great region. With over 40 museums and historic sites showcasing the rich multicultural heritage, the Kalyna Country Ecomuseum is definitely a wonderful and unique spot.

BIG GARGANTUAN & RIDICULOUSLY OVERSIZED

Mozzy the Mosquito

Home to some large petrochemical companies, Rainbow Lake, situated in the northeast corner of Alberta, has many oil derricks and donkeys scattered throughout the area. One oil donkey is just a wee bit different from the others. Someone, and it wasn't me in case the police are looking, has decorated it to look like a giant, yet friendly, mosquito.

Equipping the unused oil donkey with a set of black wings, a couple of antennae and a long stinger adds a bit of colour to an otherwise boring sight. With huge, bulbous, painted eyes, Mozzy looks friendly, but I'd hate to get stung by him. I could handle losing the blood; it's the itching and scratching afterwards I could do without.

LAKE LOUISE
BANFF NATIONAL PARK

When the wind blows through Lake Louise, the lights and computers are up and running and it's business as usual at the Fairmont Château Lake Louise. In 1999, this grand hotel in the Canadian Rockies opted for "green power," and since then, it has been using wind and "run of river" power for 40 percent of its energy.

By using green power to run its 249 check-in computers, the hotel will reduce greenhouse gas emissions by nearly 100 tonnes over the course of a year. The project, spearheaded by the Pembina Institute, a non-profit group whose mandate is to encourage "sustainable energy solutions," is a leading example of why Alberta is special. Since 1999, many more Fairmont hotels have begun using wind power for their check-in terminals.

MEDICINE LAKE
JASPER NATIONAL PARK

Medicine Lake, located in Jasper National Park, is one of the most interesting and unique lakes in the province. David Copperfield would love this lake because it is magic. The lake disappears in the winter only to re-emerge the following spring. Magic, voodoo or just an act of nature? Read on to find out.

Glacier meltwaters feed into Medicine Lake, filling and often overflowing it during the summer months. But as fall creeps into winter, the lake dries up, revealing a barren mud flat with scattered ponds and a tiny creek that runs…nowhere.

Truth be told, the water drains from the bottom of the lake like a giant bathtub. And we're talking about a much bigger bathtub than even Meatloaf would need. The Maligne River flows in from the south and drains out through tiny sinkholes in the bottom. The water then flows through a cave system formed in the soluble limestone rock, only to reappear in the Maligne Canyon some 16 kilometres downstream.

During the summer months, there is so much water that the sinkholes fill too quickly and the area overflows. But as the water levels decrease and the cooler weather hits, the lakebed dries up and the river mysteriously disappears. This is one of the Western Hemisphere's largest sinking rivers and may be (though it would be hard to find out, because it is inaccessible) the largest inaccessible cave system in the world.

MILK RIVER RIDGE
RAYMOND

This is a place I can completely understand. This ridge, located just south of the town of Raymond, is actually a continental divide; not *the* Continental Divide that acts as Alberta's border with British Columbia, but a divide nonetheless. Water on the north side of the ridge flows north into the Old Man River, while water on the south side of the ridge flows south into the Milk River and then on to the Missouri River.

This complete disregard for direction appeals to me and my tendency to get lost. The river doesn't seem to know if it's coming or going.

"BIG ROCK"
OKOTOKS

They have a special rock in Okotoks. Even the name *okotoks* means "rock" in Blackfoot. This rock I'm speaking of, affectionately called the "Big Rock," is the largest erratic in North America. Take a visit and see why.

An erratic is a rock that has been moved and deposited by a glacier. This particularly big piece of pebble is located 7 kilometres west of Okotoks and has picnic sites so you can dine under its shade. Having resided in the area for over 10,000 years, it's not in much of a hurry to move.

The rock also has strong historical significance. It was once a buffalo rub, used by the animals to remove parasites or winter coats, and it is an object revered in Native legend.

And Speaking of Big Rocks...

The Big Rock Brewery located in Calgary took its name from the Okotoks Big Rock. The owner and founder of the brewery, Ed McNally, decided that the name would bode well for his brewery as the Big Rock had stood the test the time, was a local phenomenon and sounded short and snappy. Big Rock Pale Ale was introduced in 1986, and it's been smooth sailing ever since. An Alberta beer as unique as Alberta.

Very Spooky,
But Not If You're Really
Tough Like Me!

Alberta has several places that will give thrill seekers a rush.
But Alberta also has many places that will give people chills.
From obscure sightings to certified ghost towns and
ghostly bellmen wandering the halls of prestigious hotels,
Alberta has ghosts.

GHOST TOWNS

ANTHRACITE
BANFF NATIONAL PARK

Although it no longer exists, Anthracite was a small coal-mining town about 6 kilometres northeast of the town of Banff. On the south side of the Trans-Canada Highway, tourists can see the remains of the town's commercial building, the only remains visible under the shadow of Cascade Mountain.

Across the highway, tourists can still see huge coal slacks that were left behind when the mine closed. But what makes this little ghost town different from the countless others that litter the Alberta countryside?

In 1997, a former park warden told authorities that back in the 1960s he'd heard about an unmarked grave in the townsite—the grave of a child who had drowned in the Cascade River some 100 years earlier.

An investigation was done, a gravesite was discovered and the park put up a historical marker. This marker gave some small recognition to Anthracite, which was once an important coal-mining community for the entire Bow Valley. Some secrets, I guess, aren't meant to be heard.

BANKHEAD
BANFF NATIONAL PARK

From death, we often find life, and this was the case for Bankhead. As the town of Anthracite was dying, Bankhead rose to life only 2 kilometres farther north in the Cascade Valley. Today, with help of Parks Canada, visitors can walk along its ruined remains and get a close look at coal-mining town operations.

The mine produced poor-quality coal, which led to its closure in 1922, when many of the town folk packed up and left for other towns. Some chose Banff, only 7 kilometres away.

The government has built a fantastic educational exhibit in the old transformer building. This exhibit covers geology, the mining operation and the community. An old story says the last resident of the town was a Danish caretaker who made sure people weren't stealing anything from the four remaining houses.

Today, a sign and a Union Jack pay tribute to the miners who gave their lives in France and Belgium during the First World War.

BEAVER MINES
PINCHER CREEK

Beaver Mines sprung up when coal was found in Beaver Creek, 24 kilometres west of Pincher Creek. The Western Coal and Coke Company began developing the site in 1911. By 1912, a town of 1000 had been built, with stores, hotels and high-quality homes. At its heart were the 450 miners employed by the mine.

Unfortunately, Beaver Mines met the same fate as most mines in the region. Strikes during World War I hindered production, and when trains switched to diesel fuel, 75 percent of Alberta's coalmines were put out of business.

Beaver Mines did not die quietly and officially shut down in 1971. The mines may have closed, but people still call Beaver Mines home today.

BITUMONT
FORT MCMURRAY

Possibly the first location of the oil sands up near Fort McMurray, Bitumont is all but deserted now and has been closed off due to danger risks. And perhaps a few ghosts.

Looking to strike it rich, Robert C. Fitzsimmons of Edmonton went to an area about 90 kilometres north of Fort McMurray, which had "huge pools of oil." His plan didn't materialize, at least not overnight. He took over the site in 1923 and finally, in 1930, his small operation produced 300 barrels of bitumen during the summer months.

Funding was a constant problem, and by 1932, Fitzsimmons had spent nearly $200,000 trying to keep the oil sands project running. Between 1932 and 1937, the plant didn't function, as his sources of capital had all run dry. In 1941, he sold the plant to another entrepreneur, L.R. Champion, and the name was changed to Oil Sands Limited.

Try as he might, Champion couldn't make the plant profitable, even with his idea for a separation plant. By 1948, the provincial government had taken over the proprietorship of the plant, only to sell it in 1955.

Three years of frustration later, the plant closed for good. It took 16 years for it to be deemed a Provincial Historic Site and it's now run by Alberta Community Development. Despite all its hardships, the Bitumont site was the first commercial oil sands separation and refining operation to be established.

Today, buried amongst the trees up north, the plant still stands, an eerie reminder of what could have been. The death of an industry still hangs over the buildings that remain.

BIG
GARGANTUAN & RIDICULOUSLY OVERSIZED

Swan and Grizzly

Known for the grizzly bears that inhabit the area, Swan Hills has a unique roadside attraction: a statue of a grizzly bear that captures the animal's fury, strength and awesome power. And standing up to the bear is the statue of a mother swan, protecting her eggs. But before you put all your money on the bear, keep in mind that swans can be rather intimidating. Located at the Swan Hills Tourism Booth, the statue fills residents of the town with great pride. It is an impressive site for visitors when they first enter the town. Built to showcase the rugged and natural beauty of the area, the statue took over 500 hours to build. Edmonton artist Kevin Oracheski used over 20,000 pieces of metal to construct the statue. Oracheski is one of only a handful of artists throughout the world who uses such a technique, and his statue is both impressive and unique.

THE TOWN THAT WAS, THEN WASN'T, THEN WAS...

BRULE

This is the story of a town that was and then wasn't but is again. Back in 1912 the town of Brule was established to furnish coal for the Canadian Northern Railway. When World War I broke out, Brule was booming. During its peak in the 1920s, Brule housed around 500 people who could entertain themselves at a theatre, a golf course and even at the racetrack.

And then it was over. The seam of high-quality coal dried up and there was nothing left to do but close the mine down. The end finally came in 1928 when the former miners and their families packed up and left town, looking for work in other mining communities.

By 1932, the 100 or so buildings left were empty and deserted; only the ghosts of the past remained. Board by board, house by house, the town was taken apart and the lumber hauled some 320 kilometres north to Edmonton to build a series of cottage-style houses.

But the town had plans for another life, and slowly it rose from the nothingness that once was and returned—not quite with a fervour, but it returned. Today, only a few people live in the once-deserted ghost town, but they are happy with their peaceful existence. Talk about here today, gone tomorrow and here today again.

EAST COULEE
DRUMHELLER

Only 16 kilometres from Drumheller, East Coulee is probably the best-preserved coal-mining ghost town in Alberta. Visitors can still see the eight-storey tipple that provides glorious views of the mine site and the Drumheller Valley. Complete with an old miner's shack and office, which contains original documents from over 140 mines, this mine site/ghost town is one to be seen.

Once a thriving community of over 3000 people, East Coulee barely hangs on these days with a few more than 200 people calling it home. But just east of the town is the recently restored historic Atlas Coalmine, which tourists come to visit.

While many of the old buildings are withered and decaying, the town folk have turned the old school into a museum offering up some history on East Coulee. During the mine's prosperous years, from 1928 to 1955, it was churning out hundreds of thousands of tonnes of coal per year. Now, that is little more than history, but history well preserved.

EAST COULEE'S OLDEST COAL MINE CANARY

LITTLE CHICAGO/LITTLE NEW YORK
LONGVIEW AREA

Almost overnight, these two towns grew from the discovery of oil in the area, and almost as quickly, they were gone. In 1936, the area was little more than prairie farmland, but after oil was found in 1937, people began to flock there. Fuelled by years of suffering from the depression, they came so quickly that buildings just popped up like mushrooms.

Men with no money or possessions were finally earning a living. And then it was over. Little Chicago is no longer, and little remains to show it even existed. Little New York had a brighter future; it is now Longview, a quiet foothills town with a population of around 300. And instead of oil, Longview has moved on to beef jerky.

BIG

GARGANTUAN & RIDICULOUSLY OVERSIZED

"Big Sky Outdoor Layout" Railway

I was one of those little boys who had a toy train set. It was an HO scale model, and my dad made a little mountain pass out of plaster and painstakingly laid the track around, under, through and over it so the train didn't just putt around in a circle. I didn't really appreciate the work that went into such a toy, but those connected with the Big Sky Outdoor Layout model train centre would.

The hobby is called "Garden Railroading," and the site at Nanton offers Canada's largest outdoor track. With an area of over 650 m² and with over 1067 metres of track, the layout includes a 2.7-metre-high mountain, several tunnels and bridges, a lake and a mountain stream.

With two layouts to choose from, a North American and a European, visitors will be pleased to know that changes to the layout and design happen yearly, meaning there is always something new to see. And for the kids, there's a special "Thomas" play area, based on the television show *Thomas the Tank Engine*, which has captivated children for many years. Ringo Starr and George Carlin do not make any appearances in the play area, however.

MOUNTAIN PARK
JASPER NATIONAL PARK

With the Rocky Mountains providing a picturesque backdrop, Mountain Park gets my vote as the prettiest location for a ghost town. Located just outside the eastern border of Jasper National Park, Mountain Park became incorporated in 1911 and only three years later was supplying good quality coal with help of the newly formed railway.

As the coal business grew, the town prospered, eventually becoming home to nearly 1500 residents. But coal mining wasn't the only thing the town was becoming known for. Local hockey, soccer and baseball teams were outstanding, and they often fielded some of the finest athletes around, despite the obstacles of playing at 1890 metres above sea level.

Everything about the town screamed class, from the hospital, churches and school, to the library and hotels. In fact, the town could afford to recruit the best teachers possible for its four-room school, as well as the doctor and nurses for the hospital. Life in Mountain Park was very good. Unfortunately, it wasn't meant to last. The popularity of diesel as a fuel, as well as natural occurrences such as floods, helped bring a glorious run to an end. The mine closed in 1950, and within a few years the residents had left, leaving the empty buildings for the vandals or the scrap heap.

With only a few scattered remnants of civilization left for visitors to see, some former townsfolk, family and friends, have taken it upon themselves to restore the town cemetery. They erected a plaque to honour the town, the mine and the people, and they keep the cemetery painstakingly clean, as a final resting place for many of Canada's fallen World War I soldiers. It's the least this town deserved. The graveyard, by the way, just so happens to be the highest in elevation of any graveyard in the British Commonwealth.

NORDEGG

Nordegg is another of the so-called coal mine ghost towns that dot the Alberta landscape. But this one is a little different. From time to time, the silence in the area is interrupted by an eerie, droning hum. Could it be the ghosts of miners past? Back on Halloween in 1941, an explosion ripped through the mine and killed 29 workers. Could their spirits be warning people to stay away? Sadly, no. The wind plays tricks when it hits the outside walls of the freestanding buildings that mark the site.

The mine ceased its operations in 1955, and for a time during the 1960s it became a minimum-security penitentiary where prisoners were allowed to walk around freely and sleep in the old miners' boarding house—a building that still stands today.

Back in the early 1980s, a movement was passed to save the town and preserve its rich historical character. Now, the location is a haven for ghost town hunters since many of the original buildings still stand, and the old "garden city" street system is still visible, though fading with time.

SILVER CITY
CASTLE MOUNTAIN

Long before Silver City became a cinematic marvel in West Edmonton Mall and other cities throughout Canada, it was actually home to quite the astonishing tale of skullduggery.

With more in common with the Bre-X mining company than movies, Silver City sprung up in the shadows of Mount Eisenhower, more commonly known as Castle Mountain.

Back in 1881, a member of the Stoney tribe had a piece of rock analyzed, and it was found to contain copper and lead. A claim was made at Copper Mountain, across from Mount Eisenhower, and a town, Copper City, sprang up.

Almost immediately it grew to 3000 people thanks to the arrival of Canadian Pacific Railway, and the town's name was changed to Silver City—perhaps to complement Golden City (now Golden) in British Columbia.

For such a large town it was odd that Silver City had no dance halls, churches or schools. No less than six hotels with casinos and pool halls graced the streets of Silver City, and oddly enough, less than 12 women ever lived there.

But why, you ask, is it like the Bre-X scandal? Well, in 1885, the Homestakes Mines was founded by two gentlemen, Patton and Pettigrew. The mine was said to hold a large gold discovery. Soon, over 2000 shares were sold at $5 a share. So, as the shareholders were searching the mine for gold, Patton and Pettigrew fled the country. The mine turned up no gold, and Patton and Pettigrew never turned up again either. They say history repeats itself, but shouldn't we learn?

WAYNE
DRUMHELLER

No, this does not refer to the first name of the hockey player who terrorized Calgary fans throughout most of the 1980s. This refers to the town that lies 16 kilometres south of Drumheller.

Wayne is separated from Drumheller by many single-lane wooden bridges, and if you haven't crossed 11 of them, you haven't yet reached Wayne. Once you arrive in Wayne, the virtual ghost town of 40 people, you'll think you've stepped back in time.

The three-storey Last Chance Saloon in the Rosedale Hotel, which has stood in Wayne since 1913, has changed little, except for the ghost that inhabits it. Believed to be the former owner of the hotel, the ghost does little to attract attention. He just sits and bides his time, smoking his pipe, creating more of a friendly than fiendly atmosphere.

Next time you're in Wayne, offer up a cigar and see if he accepts. He may oblige you with a puff from his pipe.

GHOSTS AND CREEPY CRAWLIES

THE BANFF MERMAN
BANFF

Mountain peaks, silt-blue lakes and an abundance of wildlife draw thousands upon thousands of tourists a year to this charming hub in the Rocky Mountains. But a little off the beaten path in the town itself is one of the creepiest and most interesting tourist attractions in the province.

In the Indian Trading Post, which has been operating in Banff for over 100 years, you will find all the traditional souvenirs associated with Banff: fake bear pelts, postcards and t-shirts, plus a few Native headdresses, moccasins and blankets. But those are of little interest here.

Deep within the bowels of the store, on the left-hand side of the back room, sits a glass case with a monstrosity encaged. The Merman has been delighting, disgusting and leaving tourists speechless for many years. Photos are hard to get since the glass causes quite the glare, but the store's postcards are to die for. The Merman is lying in front of a glacial lake with a snow-capped mountain in the background, the sun shining off its scales and teeth. Definitely not something you'd take home to Mom.

But can the Merman be that hideous? Aren't all mermaids and mermen beautiful creatures? With wiry tufts of blondish white hair hanging from his gaunt face, the Banff Merman is anything but beautiful. His body is skeletal, and his sharp, pointy teeth are bared, revealing an intent that doesn't appear friendly. Love and hope do not resonate from him; more like fear and doubt. Feel free to form your own opinion, but don't say you haven't been warned.

PRINCE HOUSE, CALGARY HERITAGE PARK
CALGARY

Canada's largest living historical village is also home to the Prince House, apparently haunted by a ghost on the third floor. According to park workers, the door to the third floor is always locked and out of bounds because the stairs are too narrow for people to climb. While the explanation offered by park workers may be valid, many visitors to the park, especially those who have heard the rumours about the ghost, tend to roll their eyes when they hear it. The thought of a ghost, or the hope of a ghost, has them more intrigued than a narrow staircase.

Peter Prince built the house in 1894, and over the years he had four wives. Perhaps, when the house was relocated to the park in 1964, one of the wives decided to come with it. Prince's second wife suffered from tuberculosis and it is said, although there is no proof to confirm the information, that she was confined to the third floor because of her illness. It might be she who illuminates the third floor even though it has no lights to turn on. The park's manager has seen the rooms on that floor illuminated, as have several guards. And if that isn't enough for you, a guard dog on premises often slinks by the building with his tail between his legs. Not exactly the sort of behaviour a comfortable dog displays.

The park staff has a sense of humour about the ghost, and every Halloween they string up a sheet on the third floor and move it across the window like a ghost.

If you want to believe that the door to the third floor is locked because of a narrow staircase, by all means do so. I for one like the ghost story.

BIG
GARGANTUAN &
RIDICULOUSLY
OVERSIZED

Crown the Beaver

Sometimes, the name of a town lends itself to a mascot. Such is the case with Beaverlodge, located in the Peace Country. Given that most Albertans have seen a beaver in the wild before, and most tourists would at least know what a beaver looks like, the town chose the animal as its mascot, and hired Heavy Industries out of Calgary to build its likeness. This project resulted in "Crown," a 1360-kilogram, 4.6-metre-tall beaver sitting on a 6-metre-long log. Heavy Industries created a metal frame, covered it with expanded polystyrene (EPS) foam and then hard coated it with polyurea, to make "Crown" durable in the harsh Peace Country winter months. The scanning and milling process used to create the world's largest beaver took 432 litres of polyurea, approximately 60 litres of paint and 18 blocks of foam to make.

Standing next to Highway 43, the beaver is impossible to miss for those travelling past and through Beaverlodge. The only question that remains is, how many trees would it take to build a lodge for such a beaver?

A FAMILY GHOST
FISH CREEK PROVINCIAL PARK
CALGARY

Fish Creek Provincial Park is located in southwest Calgary and contains miles of hiking trails in a peaceful setting within the bustling city. The park is Canada's largest urban park, and much of it remains unspoiled by the city that expands and creeps around it.

This tale is not found in any books, magazines or newspapers, and it made a believer of me where ghosts are concerned. It was on a footbridge in this very park that I saw a ghost.

I was in my early 20s, walking with my best friend, killing time. We used to frequent the park when we wanted to be serious, to talk about stuff other than drinking beer and playing soccer. Some of our most brilliant ideas were born on the paths of that park, as well as a moment I will never forget.

We were leaning against a rail on a footbridge over the creek, my friend smoking, watching the snow drift onto the thin ice on the creek below. It was early fall. The air was crisp and the snow was that soft kind that barely sits on the ground and grows like cotton balls. We had seen few people all morning, not surprising as it was a weekday and we were spending our "finding-a-job" time walking in the park.

I heard my friend say "hello," and I turned to see an elderly lady with a dog walking towards us across the bridge. I said hi, she likewise, and as she crossed the bridge I noticed my friend was pale. He asked me if I believed in ghosts, and I told him, "Why not." He smiled and said, "We've just seen one."

He said the lady was his grandmother who had died five years earlier. She was wearing the exact clothes that she had worn the last time he saw her alive. I was reluctant to believe him, so he lit another cigarette and asked why she'd left no footprints on the path leading to the bridge. He was right. No footprints were left on the light dusting of snow covering the path. Later that day, he showed me a photograph of his late grandmother wearing the same outfit as we saw her in that day.

My friend still lives in Calgary and says he's seen and felt his grandmother's presence in the park since that day. She used to visit the park almost daily when she was in Calgary, so why wouldn't she want to visit it now?

THE TURTLE MOUNTAIN HOOKER
CROWSNEST PASS

It might not be the wind you hear on your next visit to the Crowsnest Pass. Even though your hair may stand up, there might just be a different reason for your follicle reaction. You may be hearing the moans of Turtle Mountain's bejewelled hooker, Montie Lewis.

One evening back in 1907, a North-West Mounted Police officer was walking by Montie's house and noticed the lights on and the door wide open. Montie was known as a "lady of the night," and seeing the house the way it was, the Mountie went looking for Montie. He found her in bed, where she made her living, but she was not living when he found her.

You don't get to be known as a bejewelled hooker without a love of jewels, and Montie wore hers all the time. When the Mountie found her, she had been stripped of them. They had a suspect— a man who was staying with her—but he was never found or tried and the jewels were never recovered.

Is Montie out looking for her missing jewels? Is she looking to once again be employed in the world's oldest profession? Could she be calling out through the Pass for possible suitors? Next time the wind blows, perhaps you'll hear your own answers.

EDMONTON GHOST TOURS
EDMONTON

The Old Strathcona region in Edmonton is rumoured to be full of ghosts, specters and the unknown. Many spooky apparitions seen there led to the start of Edmonton Ghost Tours, a spooky tour through the Old Strathcona area, complete with interesting and humourous accounts.

Nadine Bailey acts as the Ghost Host, and has done so for a few years. She entertains her guests and keeps them moving on the hour-long tour, exploring the back alleys and nooks and crannies where the ghouls and ghosts haunt.

Included in the tour is a stop at the Princess Theatre, built in 1915. According to the legend, a young projectionist was hard at work in the projection room above the second balcony when the strangest thing happened: there was a knock at the window. Without a ledge, the person knocking must have been hovering 6 metres off the ground.

FAIRMONT HOTEL MACDONALD
EDMONTON

At the Fairmont Hotel Macdonald (and you'll notice that the Fairmont Hotels are mentioned frequently in this book), strange noises have been heard in the basement and on the top floor. Legend has it that some workhorses died in the basement back in 1915, when the majestic hotel was being built. From time to time over the last 90 years, employees have heard the distinct "clip-clop" sound of hooves emanating from the basement. Either some ghostly stallions are still around, or those comedic fools from *Monty Python* are sitting in the basement banging coconut halves together. But that doesn't explain why some people have heard a carriage racing across the top floor. And somehow, I don't think it's room service.

FAIRMONT BANFF SPRINGS HOTEL
BANFF

Fairmont hotels seem to be favourite hiding spots for ghosts. The Banff Springs Hotel was originally built in 1888 by the CPR and only accessible by rail, but it was refurbished in the 1920s.

Built to resemble a Scottish baronial castle, the beauty of the hotel is matched only by its history, which includes a wonderful ghost with a tragic tale, even for a ghost. She appears in her wedding gown and begins to descend the stairs. Her train gets caught on a huge candelabra and her dress catches on fire. Understandably, she panics and rolls down the stairs. The lucky guests who get to see this apparition see her as she appeared when she died. Some guests recall sitting in one of the chairs throughout the hotel and having a bride appear beside them. The story goes that she broke her neck upon landing at the bottom of the stairs, and she's haunted the hotel ever since.

Sometimes, guests may be helped by a ghostly bellman who will take their luggage and then disappear without asking or expecting to be tipped. With such quality service from the undead, it's no wonder the Fairmont Banff Springs is world renowned.

THE EMPRESS THEATRE
FORT MACLEOD

In the tiny town of Fort Macleod, south of Calgary on Highway 2, stands a grand theatre that dates back to 1910, when Fort Macleod was going through its boom period. Standing on Main Street, the Empress Theatre has long been a focal point of the community, and has acted as a vaudeville house, concert hall, lecture hall, live theatre and finally a motion picture house.

The house is also home to a spirit that continually appears for customers and employees alike. Some say the ghost is that of Dan Boyle, former owner of the theatre, who just refuses to leave and continues to keep an eye on his beloved theatre. Others believe it is the ghost of "Ed," a former janitor who had a second job at a local auction market and liked to smoke and drink once in a while. This theory is more popular, as many sightings of the ghost are accompanied by the smell of alcohol and tobacco.

So what does the ghost do at the Empress Theatre? Does he jump on stage, do a little song and dance and leave after rapturous applause? No, but performers have seen the ghost standing on and off the stage during performances. Ed has been seen in the mirrors of the bathroom but is never there when the patrons who spot him turn around. Ed, it appears, is either pretty quick or just not there.

Plus, Ed gets up to the usual ghost stuff. Lights are turned on and off, and empty popcorn buckets somehow get removed from garbage cans and end up back on the floor. Ed is also noisy, and one concession staff worker has claimed to hear footsteps coming up from the basement and over to the concession, stopping right beside them. But Ed is apparently shy, and wasn't visible to the concession worker at the time.

No one knows if Ed prefers action movies to romantic comedies, but I'm guessing he could have bonded with Patrick Swayze in *Ghost*.

RED DEER'S GHOSTS
RED DEER

Red Deer is a delightful community just about halfway between Edmonton and Calgary on the Queen Elizabeth II Highway. And wouldn't you expect a delightful town to incorporate ghosts in a delightful way.

Red Deer's downtown core has often been inundated with sightings of ghosts, so the Downtown Business Association created a ghost collection of bronze statues that attracts thousands of visitors a year.

The statues are designed to showcase the vibrant history of Red Deer, and they offer a glimpse of the people who made Red Deer what it is today. These aren't your typical ghosts, but the statue of Reverend Gaetz is apparently a really good listener, and sometimes he'll even respond.

Perhaps the sight of a one-armed man trying to desperately control his team of horses will conjure up your own images and remembrances of power and futility. Or maybe the sight of the lone soldier standing in the middle of Ross Street, staring back at the restored train station, will inspire you to reflect on the soldier's first few steps back on his home soil. Each of the six statues has its own story to tell. And each of these stories is worth hearing.

Visitors can follow a tour and see all eight life-sized statues, including that of Francis the Pig, who escaped from the slaughter. Come to Red Deer and see the ghosts. Bring your camera; you'll actually capture these ones on film.

MULTICULTURAL HERITAGE CENTRE
STONY PLAIN

The visitors who frequent the halls of the Multicultural Heritage Centre aren't necessarily alive anymore. In the main building, formerly the old high school, ghosts can be seen walking the halls, and occasionally, white figures pop up in the shadows.

Many of the strange occurrences have been blamed on renovations to the building. When the new kitchen in the basement was built, things began to disappear only to turn up again later. Even on nights when no one is around, stools mysteriously end up on tables. Every so often, when the building is crowded, a woman in early-1900s dress appears for the slightest of moments.

In the second building, "George," as the staff calls him, likes to walk the halls with his heavy footsteps on quiet days. George also has the habit of removing objects when people are in the Opperhauser House. The Opperhauser House belonged to a prominent Stony Plain family and was built in 1910. The Opperhausers owned and operated the first general store in Stony Plain. Look to the windows, you just may see some faces looking back. If you dare, that is.

UKRAINIAN HERITAGE VILLAGE

Drive west of Edmonton on the Yellowhead Highway and you will find this turn-of-the-century historical museum, which honours its Ukrainian past. You will find everything to remind you of the early settlers, and maybe even a few of them who remain to haunt their old haunts.

Perhaps the best of these ghosts is the old wagon master who pulls his phantom wagon through the town. He rides through town, hailing his workers to go for a ride with him. Where is he going? No one has yet accepted a ride.

BIG
GARGANTUAN &
RIDICULOUSLY
OVERSIZED

Paddy the Beaver

Alberta loves beavers, and the town of Castor was actually named after the beaver. The French word for beaver is *castor*, so the town deciding on a beaver as its mascot was like me asking for a second helping of dessert at every meal: natural. Located some 160 kilometres east of Red Deer, Paddy is awaiting your visit.

While you might think that a 1.5-metre-tall beaver named Paddy isn't exactly the weirdest thing you will ever see travelling across Alberta, perhaps the wall-length mural behind him will change your mind.

As Paddy sits gnawing on the chiselled stump of cedar with his sharp teeth, a sprawling lake scene complete with beaver dam, a couple in a canoe and some fantastic landscape stretches across the stone wall behind him, portraying an idyllic setting in which to spend an afternoon or a lifetime. The stump was added to the statue at a later date but looks completely natural, like it had been there from the beginning. It's a shame that the mural is in the middle of town. I'm sure camping is not permitted in a city parking lot.

MYSTERIOUS AND HISTORIC

CASTLE MOUNTAIN
BANFF NATIONAL PARK

Even though World War I was being fought on foreign shores, some people in Canada felt that it might be best to keep tabs on those who may have had ties with the enemies. Thus, an internment camp was set up at Castle Mountain.

Under the Canada War Measures Act, more than 8000 "enemy aliens" were put into 24 different internment camps. Nearly two-thirds of these people were of Ukrainian decent. The Castle Mountain site was one of two in Banff National Park and was used as the summer camp, while the camp at the Cave and Basin was the winter camp. Conditions in the camp have been described as grim and harsh, with at least one reported suicide and over 50 escape attempts.

The camp housed as many as 600 inmates and 180 guards, and the inmates were put to work building a road from Banff to Lake Louise for 25 cents a day. The Cave and Basin inmates also had golf course expansion and bridge-building duties to look forward to.

Both camps closed in 1917, and the remaining 47 prisoners were sent to a camp in Ontario. Evenually, the camp was dismantled and left to blend in with the other ghost towns in the mountains. Over two decades ago, a poplar cross 3.5 metres tall and 1.5 metres wide was erected in a concrete base near the highway to remind visitors of this tragic event in Canadian history. The cross was torn down, but under heavy lobbying by the Ukrainian Canadian Congress, the federal government agreed, in 1994, to erect a memorial and statue near the site of the camp.

The actual camp site is hidden from the road by forest, and the government doesn't advertise its exact location for fear of looters. But if one stumbles across it, there are some remains left to see.

COFFIN HANDLE BUTTE
MILO

A young boy saddled his horse, mounted and rode out to the cattle to bring home a few stragglers. In doing so, he was never seen again. Down near Milo, some 60-odd kilometres east of High Level in southern Alberta, the tale of this young boy has been told for years.

The boy went out as a blizzard raged, and what exactly happened can only be conjectured. The story goes that the boy and his horse struggled through the biting wind, the blinding snow and the unforgiving prairie landscape. They wandered all night and into the next day. By then the boy, more than half frozen and riding a spent horse, pushed on up a gentle hill some 64 kilometres from home. He reached the east end of the butte, could go no farther and fell off his horse. Soon after, the horse collapsed.

The weather cleared, and a search for the boy and horse started. As the winter wore on, the search widened and intensified but turned up no sign of either the boy or the horse. When spring arrived, the remains of a boy and horse were found on a distant hill.

His saddened parents could do little but buy a buckboard and coffin for their dead son and leave it on a flat rock at the east rim of the butte. In a tragic twist to the story, one of the handles broke off the coffin, and according to the legend of Coffin Handle Butte, this handle was never found but lay somewhere on the prairie.

And then the legend was proven true. On May 5th, 1990, a single coffin handle was found when locals were having a memorial service for Bob Knight, who often rode his own horse through Coffin Handle Butte.

A memorial in the form of a giant granite boulder with a plaque now marks the spot where the handle was found. A barbed wire wreath, some sage grass, rope and one of Bob's old cowboy boots—turned upside down to keep out rain and snow—complete the memorial and the legend.

THE GAOL CEMETERY
FORT SASKATCHEWAN

In the Gaol Cemetery, unknown bodies lie in peace, removed from their original burial sites. The original cemetery was located on land that was required to build a new bridge across the North Saskatchewan River, and the remains of 18 burial sites were moved to the east. Tiny metal crosses mark the small patch of land surrounded by a wooden fence on the old burial site.

Between 1916 and 1960, 29 hangings took place, and if the bodies of the condemned weren't claimed by family, or if the prisoners died of natural causes, Gaol became their final resting place.

The provincial archives can place a few names, but no one is entirely sure which prisoners are buried here. The exact number of prisoners who died of natural causes and ended up in Gaol is unknown, but former guards estimate between 12 and 20.

I just hope I'm not around when one of the ghosts comes out and tells people.

LOST LEMON MINE
CROWSNEST PASS

Somewhere in the Crowsnest Pass is a vein of gold worth millions of dollars. Of course, this is just a rumour since Alberta, on the whole, is not known for gold. Volcanic rock, which isn't common in Alberta, is best for producing gold. Finding the mine might be difficult. Avoiding the curse that comes with the mine might be worse.

Back in 1870 or thereabouts, prospectors came up from Montana. Originally looking to mine gold from the North Saskatchewan River, two of the group, Lemon and Blackjack, struck out on their own.

The two mined the river with minimal success until one day they found the gold vein. They were rich. Rich beyond their wildest dreams. Unfortunately, new riches also brought new tensions. An argument ensued about whether the two should return in the spring or camp right there. While Blackjack slept, Lemon grabbed an axe and buried it in his partner's head.

Rumour has it the event was witnessed by members of the local Blackfoot tribe, who told their chief, who in turn put a curse on the area. Cruelly, the Blackfoot were blamed for the murder.

Lemon tried to return to the mine on several occasions, but each time he could not lead the expeditions back to the site. The mystery of the curse increased when several prospectors who attempted to go to the mine without Lemon ended up dying.

So does the gold remain or not? In 1988, Ron Stewart, a geological technician at the University of Alberta, announced that he had found traces of gold in the Crowsnest Volcanics formation. After a mini gold rush, it turned out the gold was of such poor quality that it was uneconomical to mine.

The mine is still there; go ahead and look for it. If you believe in the curse, you won't be surprised if you are visited by Blackjack, complete with an axe in his head. If you don't believe in the curse, searching for the mine might just be a fun way to spend a weekend or a lifetime.

LAKE MINNEWANKA
BANFF NATIONAL PARK

Not only did the War Measures Act see the creation of internment camps, it also saw the destruction of one of the biggest coalmining towns of the early 1900s. That town was built on the shores of the original Lake Minnewanka.

The new dam was built in 1941 and the entire town was flooded. Now it lies at the bottom of the second deepest mountain lake in Canada. Our own little Atlantis, the Minnewanka townsite is a popular dive spot for scuba divers around the world.

There, beneath 18.3 metres of water, divers will see building foundations, road beds, timber bridge supports and most curiously of all, an old potbelly stove in the middle of town. The original wharf is still visible, and railway tracks and power towers add to the sunken town's appeal.

Definitely not as mysterious as Atlantis, but at least people have seen Minnewanka and keep coming back to see it again.

MOUNT EDITH CAVELL
JASPER NATIONAL PARK

Most Albertans have been to Mount Edith Cavell, but how many of us actually know the story behind the naming of the mountain? Personally, though I've spent countless hours over my summers taking in her majestic sight, including the Angel Glacier spreading her wings in a show of mercy, I've never actually read any of the signs set up for visitors to read.

Edith Cavell was a Florence Nightingale type of nurse who served during World War I. Stationed in Belgium with the Red Cross, Cavell helped hundreds of soldiers escape from behind enemy lines in Germany into Holland via the underground railroad. She was captured and executed by firing squad for her deeds. Her legacy lives on with the naming of the mountain.

After the war, her remains were brought back to England and Westminster Abbey for a service in 1919. From there, her remains were sent via special train to Norwich, and people lined the whole route, wanting to pay their respects. She now lies beneath a simple grave at the eastern end of the cathedral.

Interestingly enough, Cavell never set foot in Canada, but because she helped so many Canadian soldiers during the Great War, she deserves her tribute on our shores.

And Speaking of Mount Edith Cavell...

The mountain now known as Mount Edith Cavell was originally called *La Montagne de la Grande Traverse* by the French explorers who discovered it. When the name was changed to honour an English nurse who had never set foot in Canada, the controversy it created was incredible. The controversy still exists today among those who know and love the Rockies.

PROJECT HABBAKUK
JASPER NATIONAL PARK

In 1942, thousands of miles away, Britain was engulfed in the war effort, and more of Europe was under threat of Nazi domination. Many ideas circulated regarding how to help the Allied cause. What could be done to bring the Allies closer to victory? Of all the ideas that emerged, perhaps one involving Jasper National Park was the craziest.

Project Habbakuk was the brainchild of a scientist called Geoffrey Pyke, a scientific advisor to Lord Mountbatten. Mountbatten was a commander in the Royal Navy and his ship, the HMS *Kelly*, was famous for many victories. A favourite of Sir Winston Churchill, Mountbatten was soon named chief of Combined Operations. Mountbatten, it is said, burst into Winston Churchill's bathroom and lobbed a special piece of ice into the famed leader's bath.

But not just any piece of ice. Mountbatten threw a piece of pykrete—ice with a mixture of 14 percent sawdust—into the tub. From this tiny piece, the idea of the cool aircraft carrier was born. The structures would be unsinkable and easily repairable— just add water and freeze. The landing strips would provide a place for British aircraft to land and refuel while protecting the British ships as the journeyed across a section of ocean known as U-Boat Alley. Jasper provided the perfect place, with its seclusion in the mountains and winter conditions. In early 1943, a scaled-down version was built on Patricia Lake, but even this weighed 1000 tonnes. The landing strip stayed frozen all summer, but in the end, the cost of transporting such an enormous creation was too astronomical.

To this day, scuba divers can look at remains on the bottom of the lake.

BIG
GARGANTUAN &
RIDICULOUSLY
OVERSIZED

"Ten-Ton Toots"

Ever had a piggy bank sitting on your desk, dresser or vanity and couldn't seem to fill it up? Well, if that annoyed you, best stay away from Coleman, home of a really large piggy bank. Situated on Highway 3 at the start of the Crowsnest Pass just west of Blairmore, the town decided to use a retired engine that used to pull rail cars of coal during its 50-year service in the mines across the Oldman River from downtown Coleman, to serve as a monument to the mine and to gather loose change. Alternately called "Ten-Ton Toots" and "Dinky," it hauled over 4.5 million tonnes of coal some 290,000 kilometres from the depths of Alberta to the sunlight.

At 2.1 x 2.1 x 4.2 metres, no one is sure exactly how many coins "Toots" can hold before needing emptying. "Toots" would like to encourage all Albertans to pay him a visit and to leave a donation. When it is time to empty "Toots," I hope I'm there, to collect enough quarters to do my laundry for life.

The Greatest Ever...
At Least Somewhere

*What is it like to be the biggest
or the best at something?*

*I was once voted the person with the best chance of
looking like a Beatle (George Harrison, that is,
not the hissing kind you find in Thailand),
but I was never the best at looking like a Beatle.*

*Whether being the best makes them proud,
embarrassed, conceited or just nonchalant,
these Alberta communities all have something
they can claim to be the biggest, largest or best.*

BEST IN THE WEST

MUSEUM OF THE REGIMENTS
CALGARY

Located within the city, easily accessible from any direction and hard to miss, is the Museum of the Regiments, the largest military museum in Western Canada. At 1858 m², this is actually four museums under one roof, honouring Lord Strathcona's Horse (Royal Canadians), Princess Patricia's Canadian Light Infantry, the Calgary Highlanders and the King's Own Calgary Regiment.

Here you can appreciate Canadian military history from a Calgary perspective, through ever-changing exhibits of these regiments' flags, uniforms, weapons, documents and photographs. Lifelike permanent exhibits use some of the latest display techniques, accompanied by music and narration. Many displays include the voices of actual wartime combatants, activated when a visitor nears them. One of the most outstanding exhibits portrays the Japanese Canadians who fought bravely for Canada and the Empire in World War I, many in the 10th Battalion, which became the Calgary Highlanders.

CHUCKWAGON
DEWBERRY

Continuing the fine tradition of rodeo that helps identify some of Alberta's communities, Dewberry unveiled Alberta's largest chuckwagon at the start of its 1995 Chuckwagon Races. The chuckwagon helps define Dewberry and attract tourists.

Even though the chuckwagon is one-and-a-half times the size of an actual chuckwagon, it is fully functional. The chuckwagon is

stored in a three-sided building with an open side for access to the harness and a panel removed from another side so the length of the chuckwagon is visible for all to see. So meaningful to the town was this monument that they ordered parts in from an Amish Colony in Ontario to complete it.

The chuckwagon itself sports a plaque that reads:

Built by Moe's Wheelwright & Carriage Shop Box 62, Linberg, AB.

Another plaque on the building sheds some light on the history of the town:

Lumber, labour & siding for this building funded by Erven Garnier of Dewberry, local farmer, rancher, dealer of all sorts. Born in an old farm house 1 mile west of Dewberry, 1918. May the Lord be With You–Ervin. Pipe donated by Norcen Energy Resources.

If the chuckwagon is eventually used in a race, would Clydesdales be fast enough to compete?

GREENHOUSES
REDCLIFF

Welcome to the "Greenhouse Capital of the Prairies." At least, that's what the good people of Redcliff say. Exactly what constitutes the aforementioned title? How about having more than 20 hectares under glass or plastic houses? Talk about a big backyard and an ambitious hobby.

Long hours of sunlight, inexpensive natural gas and a proximity to the Trans-Canada Highway led to the region having the largest concentration of commercial greenhouses in Western Canada.

What would you grow if you had 20 hectares to plant? At these co-op greenhouses, cucumbers are the favoured crop, but tomatoes, peppers and, of course, flowers are grown as well. I would have opted for peas, but maybe I'm silly.

"POTATO CAPITAL OF THE WEST"
VAUXHALL

If you were the "Potato Capital of the West," what sort of celebratory tribute would you use to recognize such a feat? Maybe you could open a potato museum, proudly displaying potatoes from all over the world, including hotspots like Ireland and Idaho. Or you could opt for what actually happened in Vauxhall, and create two—yes, you read that correctly—giant potato roadside attractions.

The two potatoes, one red female named Samantha and a white male potato called Sammy, replaced the old wooden sign that let the world know about Vauxhall's claim to fame.

Samantha and Sammy seem to be having a grand old time, waving and possibly dancing on their platform, each holding one end of a sign welcoming visitors. But then again, if I was a potato and knew I wasn't going to end up as a french fry, I'd be extremely happy, too.

"MUSHROOM CAPITAL OF ALBERTA"
VILNA

When I see the giant mushrooms on display in Vilna, the "Mushroom Capital of Alberta," I can't help but think back to my youth and the lunch hours spent watching *The Smurfs*. How tall would the Smurfs be if they lived in the 6-metre-tall mushrooms that make up Vilna's unique roadside attraction? Bet you Gargamel would have an easier job finding them.

The Vilna region recognizes the mushroom because it is used in many of the dishes that the early pioneers and settlers brought with them from the old country. The town's giant replica of a *Tricholoma uspale* mushroom was spearheaded by the Vilna Lion's Club. In the year 2000, Vilna was awarded participation in the Alberta Main Street Programme, and since then, the town has seen tourism as a greater asset to its wellbeing. A few more giant mushrooms wouldn't hurt, but if the townsfolk all started wearing white pants and hats and painting themselves blue, they'd be on to something wackier than even I could imagine.

FORT MACLEOD GOLF COURSE
FORT MACLEOD

In terms of bang for your buck, Fort Macleod seems to be the place to go. Of the many, and I mean many, golf courses in Alberta, only one can boast to be the first golf course in Alberta. That golf course just so happens to be in Fort Macleod.

Golf was played in the area as far back as 1890, when the course was nothing more than a series of grassy flats near the old North-West Mounted Police base. And for you history and trivia buffs, the course is also the oldest one in Canada west of Winnipeg.

Today, the course is a nice nine-hole track that, as you can imagine, has undergone many changes in its century of play. One of my golfing buddies still uses clubs that must have been rentals from the clubhouse all those years ago.

CANADA'S BEST

"BIRD CAPITAL OF CANADA"
MCLENNAN

Located on the shores of Lake Kimiwan, McLennan calls itself the "Bird Capital of Canada." It didn't just give itself the name arbitrarily; came because of the more than 200 species of birds that choose to flock to and raise their young in the area. No less than three migratory flight paths intersect the area and provide McLennan with the largest number of shorebirds and waterfowl in North America. Of course, a town with such a claim needs a bird walk and interpretive centre, and visitors can enjoy those, too.

BIG VALLEY JAMBOREE
CAMROSE

Located some 100 or so kilometres southeast of Edmonton, Camrose has a special claim to fame: it is home to Canada's largest country music festival and North America's largest outdoor music festival.

The Big Valley Jamboree packs four days of country music's biggest and most respected acts, throws in some torrid partying, sprinkles in small-town Alberta hospitality and produces a long weekend not soon forgotten.

But the Jamboree is more than just the music. Over the August long weekend, a 162-hectare mini village erupts on the edge of Camrose, complete with a tradeshow and morning bull-riding events.

Being a people person is a must when you hit the Jamboree, for you will be surrounded by country music fans and lovers of a good time from around the world. Bring comfy clothes, some sunscreen and a loud voice if you want your "yee haws" to be heard above all the others.

CARDSTON ALBERTA TEMPLE
CARDSTON

Surrounded by some of southern Alberta's best scenery, Cardston and area offer many unique sites for visitors to enjoy. The centre-piece of the town is the Cardston Alberta Temple, the first Mormon temple built outside the U.S. It was built by Mormon pioneers who settled in the area in 1887. After 10 years of construction, the temple was finally finished in 1923. The architects were both influenced by the work of Frank Lloyd Wright, which shows in the unique appearance of the granite structure.

The Cardston Temple is one of only three such temples without spires or towers, and it served as the basic template for the Laie Hawaii Temple, which was built four years before the Cardston Alberta Temple was dedicated in 1923. More recently, the provincial government named the temple a Canadian Historical Site (1995), and a commemorative plaque recognizes it as "the first consciously modern building in the province of Alberta."

REMINGTON CARRIAGE MUSEUM
CARDSTON

Cardston is also home to the Remington Carriage Museum, North America's largest collection of horse-drawn vehicles, with over 250 carriages, wagons and sleighs. Fortunately for cleaning staff, the museum doesn't have horses posing with each vehicle, but it still draws rave reviews from visitors from all over the world.

Located only minutes away from Waterton National Park, and even further south, Glacier National Park in Montana, the museum is open seven days a week. Visitors can view video displays, see a fire hall, check out the restoration shop and, of course, go for a carriage ride. And for those who like more information with their tours, guided ones are available at no extra cost. How wonderful is that?

And Speaking of Cardston...

As if the full-size carriages aren't enough, there is also a Museum of Miniatures to visit. A retired BC Ferries Captain named Roy Wittman decided he needed a hobby and started making $1/12$-scale model Wells Fargo stages and Prairie Schooner wagons. What started as a hobby became a money-making venture for Wittman, and in 2001 he opened the Museum of Miniatures to showcase his work. With a variety of scenes and even miniature model cars to cater to a different crowd, the museum is a wonderful place to spend an afternoon.

Wittman's commitment to the museum is incredible. One diorama depicts the "Westward Ho" settlers, featuring buffalo herds, other livestock and some 150 figurines in an old west town. Each one of the handmade buildings is connected by a boardwalk, made with over 700 planks. If that wasn't enough, more than 25,000 shakes were put on each of the town's buildings, by hand. Wittman's hobby is Alberta's gain, and a world class museum.

4 WING COLD LAKE
COLD LAKE

Cold Lake boasts brilliant fishing and is home to the largest inland marina in the country, but that is not what puts Cold Lake on the map. Maverick and Goose knew about it in *Top Gun,* but they opted for the warmer climes of the southern U.S. Cold Lake is home to Canada's largest air force base, perhaps *the* air force base in Canada.

The base, known as 4 Wing Cold Lake, is an International Centre of Excellence; when you mention the fighter pilot, you have to mention 4 Wing in the same sentence. The base is home to Canada's world-class tactical fighter force training facility. Its prime location also enables the base to deploy and assist fighter aircraft faster than you can say F-18. The fighter aircraft and pilots of 4 Wing are on standby to do their duties, both domestic and international, as members of Canada's air force.

With 1.17 million hectares of almost unrestricted air weapons range space, it is no wonder that 4 Wing is Canada's largest and busiest fighter wing squadron. Such an accomplishment comes with perks, and the air weapons range is equipped with state-of-the-art threats and targets and other world-class amenities.

DIPLOMAT MINE INTERPRETIVE SITE
FORESTBURG

Forestburg, Alberta is home to the Diplomat Mine Interpretive Site. This is Canada's only surface mining museum and its star attraction is the Marion 360, North America's oldest stripping shovel. The outdoor displays explain mining on the prairies from the early "gopher hole" mines to present-day mining and reclamation.

Not far down the road, there is another mine to visit: the Luscar Ltd Paintearth Mines. This site is home to one of the largest coal shovels in the world: Mr. Diplomat, a 1465-tonne shovel that runs on electricity. Diplomat, in case you, like I, didn't know, is a trade name for coal.

CANADIAN DEATH RACE
GRANDE CACHE

Somewhere (okay, Grande Cache), someone had the idea that a marathon or a triathlon wasn't nearly dangerous, extreme or tough enough for competitors. A few locals decided to take advantage of the natural wonder that is Grande Cache's backyard and came up with a more challenging course. Many years later, the Canadian Death Race was formed.

According to the Death Race's website, a contestant must truly have the curiosity of a cat, the constitution of an ox and the spirit of adventure, although the contestant's friends and loved ones may have a completely different description of the contestant's mental health. The course is 125 kilometres long and stretches over three mountain ranges, with about 5182 metres in elevation change. Did I mention that contestants must also cross a river at the Hell's Gate canyon? With a name like the Death Race, the canyon couldn't exactly be called the Tumbling Torrents, now could it?

Proving that the founders of the race were as smart as they were fit, they threw in a bit of Greek mythology by making contestants pay a boatman to cross the river. Okay, it's a bit of dark mythology, since Charon was the ferryman of the dead, and those who didn't present him with one gold coin would have to walk the banks of the river Styx for eternity. But by now, you should get the idea that this race is one-of-a-kind in Canada.

Besides being a very tough race over unforgiving terrain, what else can you look forward to? Well, the wildlife in the area includes cougars, deer, elk and bears. That's right—bears. Grizzlies have been known to wander the hills that surround Grande Cache, and 125 kilometres is easier on them than it is on you.

So, save the first weekend of August to compete in the race, and make sure you have plenty of time during the next few months to recuperate or to break out of the hospital with the padded walls. Cause you gotta be slightly crazy to take part in this race.

HOT AIR BALLOONS
GRANDE PRAIRIE

Having hosted the Canadian Hot Air Balloon Championships twice, Grande Prairie earned the nickname the "Hot Air Balloon Capital of Canada."

Every year the Championships attract the finest balloonists in Canada, who proudly show off their skills and fill the sky with balloons of various colours and shapes. Usually alternating between eastern and western Canada each year, the Canadian Championships are often seen as great preparation for larger events like the North American Championship and the World Hot Air Balloon Championship.

Interestingly (and you might think I'm making this up but I'm not), the trophy that pilots compete for in the Championship is known as the Trumpeter Trophy. Correct me if I'm wrong, but haven't I heard the name "trumpeter" before when talking about Grande Prairie? See, I told you the swans were special.

LACOMBE CORN MAZE
LACOMBE

Just down the road from this central Alberta town is a summer and fall tourism boost known as the corn maze. People have been getting lost in this amazing (I'm refusing to let myself get carried away with puns) series of wrong turns and dead ends for nearly 10 years.

At nearly 6 hectares, the maze can provide hours of entertainment, or hair-pulling frustration. The stalks stand 2.7 metres high and the maze is divided into three sections. While the ultimate goal is to reach the exit, most of the fun is getting there, and the makers of the maze have left little passports or trivia questions to make the maze a more interactive experience. And just so you can't memorize the layout of the maze from year to year, the design changes annually. In 2005, the maze was shaped to celebrate Alberta's centennial. Guests last year had to find their way around Alberta's Coat of Arms with the words "Alberta Centennial" printed across the top. Talk about some creative people!

And Speaking of the Corn Maze…

As if one of Alberta's favourite tourist attractions wasn't enough to warrant mention, the corn maze folks have gone out and added a little piece of history to their locale. The Lacombe Corn Maze is now home to Canada's first "jumping pillow."

What exactly is a jumping pillow, you might ask? Well, a jumping pillow is hours of fun for kids of all ages. Think of a giant air sock, or a bouncy castle without the towers, walls, or crocodile-infested moat, and you're on the right path. The jumping pillow takes all the fun and bounce from the trampoline without the worries of getting caught in the springs or flying off the surface. The phenomenon has taken Europe by storm, and Lacombe has introduced the craze to Alberta and Canada. Way to go, Lacombe!

BIG GARGANTUAN & RIDICULOUSLY OVERSIZED

Cornstalk

Jack had his beanstalk, and Taberites have their cornstalk. Standing an impressive 11 metres tall, the metal cornstalk in Taber clearly symbolizes the value of the region's corn production to the town.

It is difficult to drive past a roadside turnout in Alberta during the summer and not see a trailer loaded with sweet, succulent Taber corn. Known throughout Western Canada for quality, Taber corn is a summer staple that many can't live without. And the stalks of corn that climb into the sky in Taber are a nice tribute to it.

Most Albertans have heard of Taber corn, but do most Albertans know where Taber is on a map? Follow Highway 3 east from Lethbridge heading towards Medicine Hat and you will drive right by Taber. You might as well look at the cornstalk.

Situated in front of the AquaFun Centre, the stalks, while sturdy, should not be used to climb into the sky to search for giants or other odd creatures. Now if I could only find a pat of butter large enough to match.

"NATIONAL CAPITAL OF FRENCH MURALS"

LEGAL

This town north of Edmonton is very proud of its French roots, and it received official bilingual status in 2000, only two years after officially becoming a town. But the most interesting thing about Legal, and the reason the town attracts visitors from across Canada and the world, is its claim to be the National Capital of French Murals. Right here in Alberta, a place that would make Québec jealous.

Throughout the town, visitors will spot 28 different murals depicting the history and heritage of this completely bilingual town. Legal's strong cultural heritage has collaborated with the Association canadienne-française de l'Alberta régionale Centralta to bring this project to life. The town now flourishes with a wonderful display of murals.

Historical Mural

What takes 25 sheets of 4 × 8 plywood to build? The answer is simple, really: a 30.5-metre-long mural depicting the history of Elk Point. Built in 1987, the images on the mural were researched and painted by Billie Milholland, with coordination from the Elk Point Historical Society. The mural was carefully researched and contains images that reference 80 years of history for Elk Point. The town is very proud of this unique and momentous tribute.

BEST IN THE WORLD

WORLD'S LARGEST PUTTER
BOW ISLAND

Bow Island seems to have a monopoly on large roadside attractions, with Pinto MacBean, the pinto bean mascot, a giant steel sunflower and an oil derrick. Per capita, it must rank among the highest in the world in terms of such attractions. Not wanting to be outdone, the Bow Island Golf Club had George Thacker create the world's largest putter to welcome golfers to the club.

The simple design of the putter means it could be used by both left- and right-handed giants, but details are limited about whether it conforms to the Canadian Golf Association's standards of weight and length.

OIL LAMP
DONALDA

With a warm shining light to greet you at night, Donalda is the lamp capital of the world. Not only does it boast Alberta's only oil lamp museum, but down at the end of Main Street, completely visible from just about anywhere in the province it would seem, is the world's largest lamp.

Conveniently located in central Alberta, a short drive northeast of Stettler and not too far from Red Deer, Donalda and the oil lamp should be visited by all.

Constructed of metal, concrete, Styrofoam (to prevent frost damage) and of course fibreglass, the lamp stands 12.8 metres tall. The lamp is on from dusk till dawn and powered by a 400-watt street lamp bulb.

Originally a millennium project, the lamp was delivered on June 23, 2000, set up in two hours and fully functional by June 30, 2000. The lamp, which cost an estimated $90,000—paid for by grants, fundraisers and donations—is a perfect complement to the museum.

LAMP MUSEUM
DONALDA

Donalda doesn't only have the world's largest lamp, but it also boasts Alberta's only oil lamp museum. The museum houses an impressive collection of lamps dating from the 1600s to the 1950s. Local residents Don and Beth Lawson donated an extensive collection of 500 lamps in 1979. Since that time, the number of lamps in the museum has grown to over 850. Kerosene oil lamps from the 1800s to mid 1900s make up the primary collection of lamps.

If the province ever suffered a total power outage, I'd head to Donalda; at least they'd have light.

SMITHSON INTERNATIONAL TRUCK MUSEUM
RIMBEY

Ken Smithson is a man with a passion. That passion is on display at the Smithson International Truck Museum in Rimbey, a town located west of Ponoka on Highway 53. His collection of 19 restored trucks is the most complete collection of International trucks anywhere in the world.

Smithson started this "little" project by restoring two gravel trucks, both International, until he had them in showroom condition. His next piece of work was a 1951 model he had owned previously. He bought the truck in 1981 and had it ready for the showroom by 1982. From there, the project snowballed.

In 1990, the Rimbey Historical Society purchased the collection, bought a building to house it and developed the name. And just so you know, it is hard work restoring all these old trucks—it took an average of five different trucks to supply all the necessary parts to complete one restored and ready-for-display truck. And I can't even change my oil without making a mess.

BIG GARGANTUAN & RIDICULOUSLY OVERSIZED

Slingshot

Travel southeast of Camrose on Highway 13 and you will find the tiny village of Hughenden. Not much happens in Hughenden that would scare any of the world's superpowers, but the town has decided it might be a good idea to protect itself from unsavoury guests.

Made from a single, forked tree stump, the Hughenden slingshot is armed and ready for action. The rubber shot is cocked in position to fire and held in place by a small metal rod that is stuck in the ground. And just so people know exactly where they are and why the slingshot is there, a hand-painted sign reads "Canada Strikes Back," leaving little doubt as to what we will do if ever a giant named Goliath ventures upon us.

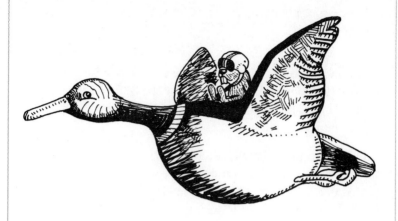

MALLARD DUCK
ANDREW

For a glimpse of a mallard duck in full flight, one doesn't necessarily have to cast one's eyes to the stratosphere. A simple drive some 105 kilometres north of Edmonton offers the chance to see exactly what that sight might look like.

Situated in the natural wetlands of north-central Alberta, Andrew is home to a giant mallard duck statue. The Alberta government gave the town a tourism grant to construct the duck, and the local Lions Club spearheaded the project.

Built in 1992 to celebrate the surrounding wetlands, including Whitford Lake, the mallard is symbolic to the region. It is a popular breeding ground for ducks, and mallards can be seen throughout summer on many of the waterways in the area.

With a wingspan of 7 metres and weighing over one tonne, Andrew's mallard duck is by far the largest of its kind. The statue captures the bird in flight, wings outstretched, long green neck leading the way. With a picnic table right underneath one of the outstretched wings, the mallard offers protection from sun and rain. That is, if the sun and rain happen to hit the duck at a particular angle. But, the chance is there, isn't it?

SUZIE THE SOFTBALL
CHAUVIN

Sometimes hosting a large softball tournament just isn't enough to put a community on the map. What else could Chauvin do to help celebrate and welcome ballplayers and visitors alike? Perhaps a giant softball would work.

And thus, Suzie was born. Measuring 1.8 metres in diameter, the softball that greets people on their drive to the softball diamonds was created in 1977 and has stood smiling ever since. Made from old fibreglass tanks, Suzie is the largest softball in the world. Not even Michael Jordan in his failed attempt at professional baseball could swing and miss if this softball was tossed his way.

WAGON WHEEL AND PICK AXE
FORT ASSINIBOINE

South of Swan Hills on Highway 33 and located within the old Fort Assiniboine stands the world's largest wagon wheel and pickaxe. This massive monument was revealed on July 20th, 2005. The wagon wheel stands 7.6 metres tall, and the axe is only slightly smaller at 6.1 metres. Hand-carved from EPS foam and hard-coated to withstand the weather, the frame is made from reinforced steel, assuring some stability.

My only question about the giant attractions revolves around how they managed to keep them hidden before revealing them to the public. They must have some really large storage sheds up in the Fort.

Grey Geese

Hanna, the "Grey Goose Capital of Canada," has three wonderful grey goose monuments around town. None of them would win any awards for largest anything, but the sight of a grey goose in flight is impressive, nearly as impressive as Hanna native, former NHLer and all-around great man Lanny MacDonald's moustache.

In fact, each monument captures the majestic grey goose in a different position: one landing, one in flight and one taking off. Visible from the major traffic ways, the geese are a terrific sight whether you are passing through town or having a picnic in one of the parks or enjoying a leisurely stroll.

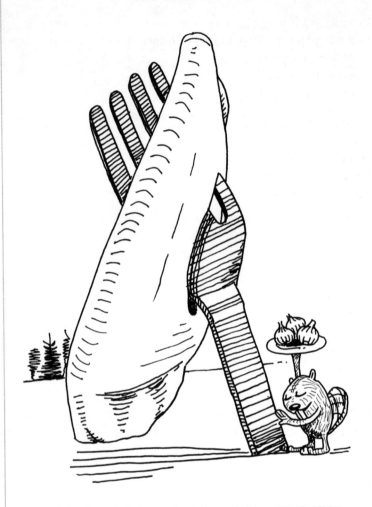

WORLD'S LARGEST PYROGY
GLENDON

Several thousand miles away from the Ukraine, but close in heart and heritage, the town folk of Glendon are the proud owners of the world's largest pyrogy. And it's not just the world's largest pyrogy, but also world famous.

In 1989, the Village of Glendon sent a notice to every business in town, asking for unique ideas to attract tourists. From all the ideas that were generated, the giant pyrogy was the one most suited to the region, and one that would be bizarre enough to act as a tourism generator.

Thanks to intense media coverage from around Canada, a special tourism grant and donations from the lottery foundation and businesses throughout the country, enough money was raised to hire contractors to build the pyrogy. Amazingly, the village still receives donations from people wanting to see their names on the plaques that sit beneath the 2722-kilogram dumpling.

The pyrogy stands 7.6 metres tall and is 3.7 metres wide with a fork skewered through the centre of it. When it was served to the public in Pyrogy Park on August 31, 1993, over 2000 people showed up to take part in the ceremony; that's nearly five times the number of people who live in Glendon. Naturally, free pyrogies were had by all, and Ukrainian dancers, musicians and a local band all provided entertainment. Plus, there was an array of souvenirs for the public to purchase. The village still receives media inquiries about the pyrogy and its effect on tourism.

Make sure you stop by Glendon for its yearly Pyrogy Festival in September, and stuff yourself silly. Or be civilized and eat until you are pleasantly full.

And Speaking of Glendon…

Did you know that one of the most interesting board games invented in 2004 can be ordered from its creators in Glendon, Alberta? The game, Mysteries of the Forest, is unique in that it seeks to educate people about the three main forest systems on the planet. By answering questions in five categories—World Forestry and Parks, Forest Sciences, General Forestry, Forest Trees and Plants and Forest Wildlife—players can learn more about the temperate rainforest, the tropical rainforest and the boreal forest. Whether you are a natural know-it-all or just want to expand your base of knowledge, this game sounds like fun. Check out their website at www.mysteriesoftheforest.com.

BADMINTON RACQUET
ST. ALBERT

The Red Willow Badminton Club needed something to bring attention to it and the sport of badminton. Since hiring swimsuit models was out of the question, constructing the largest badminton racquet in the world soon became the logical answer.

Located within sight of Boudreau Road, the racquet, at over 4 metres long, is visible from a passing car, unless of course you see the thin side first, and then you better have good eyesight. Badminton racquets aren't exactly thick objects and this one is no exception. Unfortunately, the club did not make a matching shuttlecock.

Ball and Chain Wind Gauge

Anyone who has ever been to Lethbridge knows about the wind that often rips through the coulees and valleys. I once played soccer there against Lethbridge Community College and, with the wind blowing straight into me, ran a four-minute mile. I only ran a total distance of less than 100 metres, however.

For the city's 100th birthday, the General Stewart Branch No. 4 Royal Canadian Legion, in cooperation with the Lethbridge Centennial Society, decided to erect a wind gauge. It has a ball and chain design; the ball was once used to float screens in the ocean to keep submarines from coming closer inland. The chain, naturally, is anchor chain. The ball hangs at different angles, depending on the wind.

Used to an average wind speed of just over 20 kilometres per hour, Lethbridge residents have taken to using a little humour to describe their situation. A sign reads:

When ball hangs at 22 degrees a Lethbridgian considers it "Calm."
When ball hangs at 45 degrees a Lethbridgian considers it "Fairly Calm."
When ball hangs at 90 degrees a Lethbridgian considers it "Little Windy."
When chain stretches a Lethbridgian considers it "Kind of Brisk."
When chain breaks a Lethbridgian considers it "Sure is Windy."

At the site of the ball and chain wind gauge, three time capsules were buried in 1985, the year the wind gauge was erected, to be opened in 25, 50 and 100 years. According to my basic math skills, the first time capsule will be opened in 2010, the second in 2035 and the last in 2085. I love surprises, so I'll try and attend all three, but realistically, only two are doable. These time capsules are still located at the original site of the ball and chain wind gauge—at the east end of the High Level Bridge on top of the coulees. The wind gauge now resides in front of the Visitors Centre.

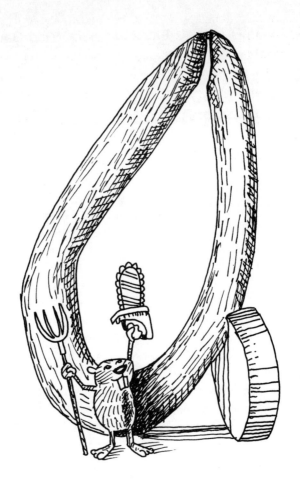

KIELBASA
MUNDARE

If Mundare and Glendon could hook up, the feast on offer would be fantastic. Mundare is home to Stawnichy's Meat Processing plant, and in honour of the outstanding sausage produced in the plant, the town erected a 12.2-metre-tall kielbasa.

Built to withstand high winds and surrounded by four flags (Canada's, Alberta's, Mudare's and Stawnichy's), the kielbasa has attracted media coverage and tourists from afar. Stawnichy's has been in Mundare for over 50 years, and the kielbasa will be there for many more.

Constructed from fibreglass, the sausage cost over $120,000 to build, making it the most expensive single ring of Stawnichy's kielbasa in the world.

Now, if I could only find some cabbage rolls, a true Alberta triple threat would be realized.

CLOCK TOWER
WAINWRIGHT

Wainwright has a unique symbol of hope sitting in the intersection of Main Street and 2nd Avenue. The world's largest known freestanding clock tower has been in Wainwright since 1925. Built as a memorial to the soldiers who lost their lives in World War I, the tower was constructed with native granite fieldstones collected by local schoolchildren and farmers. Although not ornate, the tower has simple roman lines that rise from a double platform of concrete and hold the clock some 10.7 metres above the roadway.

The four clock faces were brought from England and ran on battery power until the town started to use electricity in 1958–59, when Main Street was paved. The clock tower survived the fire of 1929, the worst fire in the history of small-town Alberta. Seventy businesses and eight homes were totally destroyed, but the tower stood alone on the road, like some strange beacon of hope that everything would rise again.

PYSANKA
VEGREVILLE

Vegreville, Alberta, and the rest of the world have the Mounties to thank for the giant pysanka, or Ukrainian Easter egg, that graces Pysanka Park in Vegreville, north of Edmonton. In 1973, the Alberta government founded the Alberta Century Celebrations Committee to honour the upcoming centennial of the Royal Canadian Mounted Police. The Vegreville town council fielded many suggestions on how to honour the Mounties, the best of which was to construct a giant Easter egg symbolizing the peace and security the Mounties had offered the area's pioneers throughout the years. True to the ancestry of many of Vegreville's residents, the decorating of eggs is a Ukrainian tradition that has impressed the world for centuries. In fact, *pysanka* is the Ukrainian word for Easter egg and comes from the verb *pysaty,* which means "to write."

No ordinary undertaking, the egg is a visual, technical and scientific marvel. Consisting of 2208 equilateral aluminum triangles, 524 star patterns, 3512 visible facets, 6978 nuts and bolts and 177 internal struts, the egg was designed by Ronald Resch, a professor of computer science at the University of Utah. The pysanka was also the first egg designed by computer modelling.

About 10 adults holding hands can surround the equator of this giant egg, and since winds in the Vegreville region can reach up to 100 kilometres per hour, the builders made the egg kinetic—it rotates, much like a weather vane.

The egg's symbolism could be covered in a separate book and my description of it pales in comparison to seeing the egg. With symbols representing life and good fortune, the Trinity, eternity, a good harvest and protection, the pysanka captures the history of the region while maintaining a strong link with the present and the future.

And Speaking of Giant Easter Eggs…

World famous and visited by thousands of tourists a year,
Vegreville's giant pysanka has even entertained royalty when,
in 1978, Queen Elizabeth II and Prince Edward paid the site
a visit. While reports of Edward searching the area for the Easter
Bunny that delivered the egg are merely hearsay, the Royals were
impressed, as is anyone who has ever seen the pysanka.

WORLD'S SMALLEST CURLING RINK
SEEBE

In the tiny hamlet of Seebe, located in the Kananaskis region, there is something of interest to anyone with sports in their blood. So impressive is the site that the *Guinness Book of World Records* has even taken notice.

Seebe is home to the smallest curling rink in the world. There is no mention if the curlers who curl at the rink are the smallest in the world, but it would probably help.

And Speaking of Rinks...

On a farm near Viking, Grace and Louis Sutter raised seven sons. Astonishingly, six went on to play in the National Hockey League. Combined, Brian, Duane, Darryl, Brent, Rich and Ron played nearly 5000 games at this highest level of hockey—and over 600 more in the playoffs. For a stretch in the early to mid 1980s, there were six Sutter brothers playing in the NHL at the same time. What a weird and wonderful legacy the Sutters have provided in putting a small Alberta town on the map.

OLYMPIC MUSEUM
CALGARY

On Calgary's west border, standing majestically at Canada Olympic Park, are the ski jump towers that visitors and citizens can spot from miles away. The site is also home to the Olympic Hall of Fame and Museum, honouring the 1988 Calgary Winter Olympics.

Over 60,000 visitors a year come to see one of the most extensive collections of Olympic artifacts anywhere in the world. With an array of torches from previous Olympic cities and video presentations that capture the excitement of "the best games ever," Canada Olympic Park, complete with the ski jump towers, provides an endearing and wonderful legacy of Calgary's shining moment.

Saamis Tipi

When the 1988 Calgary Olympics ended, the giant tri-coloured Saamis Tipi constructed for the event as a symbol of Canada's Native heritage was moved to Medicine Hat.

At well over 60 metres tall and weighing over 800 tonnes, including the base, the tipi can withstand extreme temperatures and winds of up to 240 kilometres per hour. The tipi towered over the Olympic cauldron during the opening and closing ceremonies.

Saamis (pronounced SA-AH-UMP-SIN) is the Blackfoot word for an eagle tail feather headdress (a hat worn by the Medicine Man, or a Medicine Hat). Painted white for purity, red for the rising and setting sun and blue for the flowing waters, the tipi is a spectacle for the eyes.

Like Lego and Tinker Toys, But Much More Impressive

When nature isn't carving out amazing landscapes
or getting animals to do funny things,
man often feels the need to add a few impressive,
and sometimes tacky, sights to the landscape.

Whether you need options
when you buy that next pair of boots
or need a striking way to travel across a canyon or gully,
Alberta has something for you.

BRIDGING THAT GAP

ANIMAL BRIDGES
BANFF

I was always told to look both ways before I crossed the street, but I never had to venture across four lanes of Trans-Canada Highway and hundreds of cars travelling close to 100 kilometres per hour or faster. The peril for the wildlife in Banff National Park was terrible; many animals ended up as sad displays on the side of the road.

As a solution to this problem, two tree-covered, 50-metre-wide overpasses were constructed to give the animals a natural-looking path across the highway. In addition to the overpasses, 21 under-passes were created to aid in animal and motorist safety.

Now, I can hear people complaining that the invention of the over- and underpasses has reduced their chance of seeing wild-life, but it has also cut down the roadkill and collision rates with animals by more than 80 percent. With such numbers, don't be surprised if more overpasses are created.

Curiously, cougars and black bears prefer the underground passes to the overpasses. Elk, moose, wolves and grizzly bears prefer to take the high road, and really, who's going to stop them?

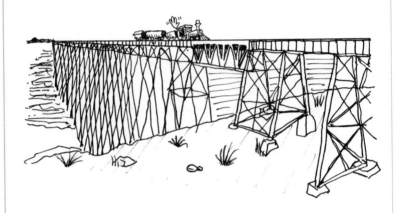

HIGH LEVEL BRIDGE
LETHBRIDGE

Lethbridge is home to one of Canada's greatest structural marvels: the High Level Bridge used by CP Rail. The bridge is the longest and highest of its kind in the world, stretching 1.6 kilometres. At over 91 metres tall, the bridge is truly an engineering wonder. Weirdly, the west end of the bridge is slightly more than 6.4 metres higher than the east end. Does that mean westward-bound trains travel a little slower as it's an uphill journey through Lethbridge? These are just little things that I think about.

DAM, THAT'S IMPRESSIVE...AND OTHER STRUCTURES

BASSANO DAM
BASSANO

The giant undertaking that was the construction of the Bassano Dam is only overshadowed by the giant service this structure provides to the Eastern Irrigation District in southern Alberta.

Bassano is located southeast of Calgary on the Trans-Canada Highway, just a few thousand wheel rotations from Brooks. The dam itself is located 5 kilometres southwest of the town.

Construction began in 1910 and was completed in 1914, the lengthy time span due in no small part to the immense size of the dam. The earthen embankment stretched some 2134 metres across, was 107 metres tall at its highest point and contained about 765,000 m^3 of earth.

The dam is vital to the survival of a region that is 400 kilometres bigger than all of Prince Edward Island. Ensuring there is enough water for 113,000 hectares of farmland, 12,000 hectares of managed wetlands and the local water requirements of businesses and consumers in an area of 20,000 people is no small feat. The dam straddles the Bow River and provides the region with just about all its water.

BIG GARGANTUAN & RIDICULOUSLY OVERSIZED

Tire Man

Located west of Lac La Biche on Highway 63, the town of Grassland has a unique humanoid with whom visitors can pose for pictures. The Grassland Tire Man always has a smile on his face, since the white painted disc that sits inside his tire head never changes expression.

No less than 17 tires make up its legs, stacked flat and supported by a frame that also connects them to a larger tire that serves as the man's stomach. Each arm has five tires, arranged from largest to smallest as they move outward. His outstretched fingers round off a unique, and rubbery, man from the north.

BROOKS AQUEDUCT
BROOKS

Long, and long unused, the Brooks Aqueduct is a hollow reminder of what used to be. Spanning 3.2 kilometres across the southern Alberta landscape, the aqueduct once shuttled water for local farm communities. Today, the aqueduct serves as a monument to those risk-takers who challenged engineering principles for the betterment of the Alberta landscape. Information is available at the aqueduct, which is now an Alberta Historic Site.

Since a shallow valley cut off the southeastern portion from the rest of the eastern valley, something needed to be done to get water across. An earthen fill was inconceivable at that time, and the ideas for siphons and pipes were rejected in favour of the elevated canal system that now stands dormant.

Although it operated from 1915 to 1979, the aqueduct never quite lived up to the promises or the hopes of its creators, who believed they could use untried engineering principles. Designed with cost-saving measures in mind, the 65-year experiment eventually failed. At the time, the Canadian Pacific Railway's Irrigation Division had constructed an engineering marvel. Today it is just a marvel to see.

CAIRNS
LAC LA BICHE

While they aren't jaw dropping in terms of size, the cairns located throughout Lakeland Provincial Park and the Lac La Biche region make jaws drop for different reasons.

The cairns are memorials for fallen airmen. Each one tells the history of a pilot and gives us a lasting legacy for the men who helped shape the country. In the 1950s, the Canadian Board on Geographical Names, as it was known back then, began to name unnamed lakes after fallen service men of World War II.

Since the majority of these cairns are accessible only by quad during the summer months, a memorial wall was erected in Lac La Biche in front of the legion to commemorate them.

David Thompson

David Thompson is responsible for mapping more than 125,000 kilometres of wilderness, and Lac La Biche is one of three towns to have statues dedicated to the young Welshman who passed through the area.

The statue, made of concrete and bronze and designed by Herman Poulin, who designed and carved other Alberta monuments, was built to celebrate Lac La Biche's bicentennial and to recognize Thompson's arrival. It has Thompson standing at the front of a canoe as he, his guide and another passenger land on the shores of Lac La Biche. The statue shows Thompson pointing to the spot where he landed all those years ago.

The plaque beneath the monument reads, "He arrives in canoe brigade at 1:00 PM, October 4, 1798, after crossing Portage La Biche. Made the final approach in a light canoe accompanied by his guide Laderoote, and someone known only as 'the Indian.'"

MALLS, MUSEUMS AND HIGH-RISES: THE URBAN JUNGLE

A SADDLE, A TOWER, A MUSEUM
CALGARY

The two most recognizable Calgary landmarks—the Calgary Tower and the Saddledome—are visually interesting and well worth a visit. The Tower enables you to walk along a glass floor and look down at the city some 160 metres below. Not exactly weird, but kind of gives you a different sort of chill. The Saddledome, home to the Calgary Flames, is aptly named as it looks like a saddle. Anything more said about the building would be silly. Picture a saddle for a really large horse and you've got it.

But Calgary does have some buildings that house impressive sites. The Glenbow Museum is Western Canada's largest cultural institution and includes a museum, an art program, a library and extensive archives. It houses displays that celebrate the diverse cultures and events that helped shape the Canadian West, including a new gallery devoted to the exploration of Blackfoot history and culture.

Thanks to places like the Glenbow Museum, Albertans might just shake the label of cowboys and oil workers. We are a province with a great diversity, and we are proud to show it.

And Speaking of Calgary...

Calgary is unique among cities, especially in Alberta, as its downtown core is connected by enclosed suspended walkways. The walkways are 4.6 metres above the ground, and 60 of them connect 100 buildings. This creates a 16-kilometre walking route that circles the core of the city, ideal for those who don't want to go outside in the colder winter months.

The path leads past shops, restaurants, through office towers and to theatres. In Calgary, it is possible to walk and shop till you drop without having to go outside at all. What will they think of next?

Spike the Mechanical Man

Spike is very tall. At over 8.2 metres, he is by far the tallest man in Calgary. Spike doesn't like rain much though, for he is made of metal. To commemorate the 75th anniversary of the Canadian Pacific Rail's Ogden Yards in Calgary, numerous tradespeople at the yards collected barrels and old freight and used them to construct the happy-looking, colourful monument that would welcome visitors for years to come. "Oggie," as he was originally named and is still called by some, stands near the entrance to the shops area of the old railyards. With his height, he can probably see the entire yard, if only he could turn around or tilt his head.

WEST EDMONTON MALL
EDMONTON

Wherever you go throughout the world, the mention of Edmonton usually brings up the question, "Is the mall really that big?" In a word, "yes." Some throw out numbers like over 20 million visitors a year (which makes it Alberta's top tourist destination), and during weekends at Christmastime, West Edmonton Mall officially becomes the third largest city in Alberta.

In case you've been living under a rock, or in case large malls are not your scene, I'll give you a brief synopsis of what you're missing. We'll start with the shopping, because after all, it is a mall and malls are made for shopping. With over 800 stores and services and over 100 eating establishments, the mall has enough sights and scenes for people to tour for weeks. But even shopping gets tiring, unless you're Paris Hilton, and West Edmonton Mall has much more to offer.

Often regarded as the "Eighth Wonder of the World," the mall contains seven attractions not necessarily associated with shopping malls. And I'm not even going to mention the NHL-sized ice hockey rink inside the mall—that seems rather mundane compared to everything else the mall offers up.

Even in the dead of winter, which in Alberta can hit in October, Edmontonians can go and relax on a beach and watch the waves come in, all the while staring at the glass roof above and watching the snowflakes fall. The two-hectare waterpark, featuring 23 slides and attractions, provides hours of fun for young and old.

And then there are the world records that West Edmonton Mall holds. Besides being the world's largest shopping mall, it also boasts the world's largest parking lot. Makes sense, but how come it always takes me forever to find parking when I'm there? Galaxyland, the indoor amusement park, is the largest indoor amusement park in the world. Our triple-loop roller coaster, the Mindbender, is the largest indoor roller coaster in the world and offers 73 seconds of pure excitement, if you like that sort of thing. The coaster has even been mentioned in Canada's top 10 roller coaster lists. Pretty impressive stuff when you think about it.

The mall has working submarines in a 220-metre-long lake that features real coral, some pieces over 2000 years old. For the cultured history buffs, the Santa Maria galleon is an exact replica of the ship that Columbus had when he sailed the ocean blue back in 1492. Dining is available on the boat, and since it doesn't move, seasickness is not a problem.

All in all, the mall has something for everyone...unless you crave peace and quiet and the relaxing confines of being alone. If that's the case, you should just stay home.

HIGH LEVEL BRIDGE WATERFALL
EDMONTON

Edmonton has the largest expanse of urban parkland in North America, and much of that land is bisected by the North Saskatchewan River. The river valley pathways are ideal for cyclists, inline skaters and joggers of all speeds. But how do they cross the river? One of the ways is via the High Level Bridge, which doubles as the Great Divide Waterfall during certain festivals throughout the summer.

To make this artificial waterfall, water is pumped from the river and shot through pipes attached to the top of the bridge under what used to be the train tracks. It delights Edmontonians and tourists alike. Having been to Niagara Falls, I can tell you that the Edmonton falls aren't quite as impressive, but they are a close second.

And while the waterfall is on, why not catch a ride on the streetcar, which crosses the river via the bridge 45.7 metres up, making it the highest streetcar river crossing. The accompanying fireworks on Canada Day would look great from that vantage point too. Except the car doesn't run that late at night and, thankfully, they gate off the top of the bridge so people can't walk across it. However, it does make for an interesting pit stop when the conductor of the street car has to open the fence and proceed with the journey. Nothing weird about that.

And Speaking of Edmonton...

Edmonton is home to the Telephone Historical Centre, which is the largest of its kind in North America and the only one in Canada. At the centre, you can take a look through an early Edmonton telephone directory or just marvel at how far the telephone has come.

BIG GARGANTUAN & RIDICULOUSLY OVERSIZED

Cowboy Boot

Although Calgary is known for the Calgary Stampede, Edmonton has a two-step up on it in the boot department. Built to promote the Western Boot Factory that used to operate at 10007–167 Street, on the corner stands a cowboy boot that's 12 metres tall and weighs 40 tonnes. The Western Boot Factory is no longer, but the boot remains, and there have been plans to add another 6 metres to its height. Whether or not that happens is up in the air. I'm waiting to find the spurs to go with the boots.

ROMAN CATHOLIC AND ANGLICAN CHURCHES

FORT CHIPEWYAN

As the oldest Euro-Canadian community in Alberta, it is only fitting that Fort Chip also has some of the oldest buildings still in use in the province, including an imposing Roman Catholic Church built back in 1909 and an Anglican Church that was established in 1874. Add to the mix a school that was built even before the Anglican Church and run by the Grey Nuns for over 100 years.

In 1998, the Nativity of the Blessed Virgin Mary Roman Catholic Church was designated a Provincial Historic Resource, followed in 2001 by St. Paul the Apostle Anglican Church, day school and cemetery—the most northerly of approximately 200 Provincial Historic Resources.

Thanks to government funding, this tiny community can maintain and improve the conditions of these three buildings and hopefully keep them in the community for another 100 years.

Interesting Trivia

Some things just need to be said. Alberta's communities are loaded with brilliant nuggets of information and trivia that scream, "Let me out, the people must know about me!"

Okay, they might not scream like that, but they should. Sit back and enjoy some of the most delightful and possibly unknown facts about Alberta.

FIRST IN CLASS, OR WE'RE JUST BETTER THAN YOU!

ATHABASCA UNIVERSITY
ATHABASCA

Since 1970, when the Alberta government decided to finally add a fourth university in the province, Athabasca University (AU) has been providing distance education to over 260,000 students from across the world.

As "Canada's Open University," AU served more than 32,000 students in 2004–05. The flexibility of the programs, the do-it-at-your-own-pace schedule and the fact that most students still maintain full-time jobs while taking courses through AU all make the university appealing.

So respected within the educational community is AU that in 2004, the International Council for Open and Distance Education awarded the university an Institutional Award of Excellence. If that wasn't enough, the MBA program was voted one of the top 75 in the world by the Financial Times of London.

The main campus moved from Edmonton to Athabasca in 1984 but still operates satellite campuses in Edmonton and Calgary. Working in conjunction with Alberta's other universities, AU looks set to lead the world in distance education for decades to come.

FIRST NORTH AMERICAN MOUNTAIN CLIMBING FATALITY
BANFF NATIONAL PARK

With all the beauty it offers, Banff has long been a place that hikers, campers and mountaineers would visit. Unfortunately, Banff is also home to the first mountain climbing casualty in North America.

When Phillip S. Abbot arrived in the Canadian Rockies in 1895, he was regarded as one of the most capable mountaineers in North America. He, Charles S. Thompson and Charles Fay soon completed the first known ascent of Mount Hector. Not stopping there, the three moved on to the Selkirk Range to continue climbing. Over that summer, the group unsuccessfully tried to climb Mount Lefroy, near Lake Louise, twice. Fay later wrote that "the fates were against us, and we withdrew, with a feeling that Lefroy was our debtor."

They returned to their homes for the winter and thought about the challenge that had defeated them. The next summer, the three returned to Lake Louise, with one aim in mind. In the early morning of August 3, 1896, the three, along with their guide George Little, paddled across Lake Louise towards Mount Lefroy. After they reached what is now known as "Abbot's Pass," the group began preparations for their climb. Abbot was full of confidence that the mountain could be taken.

Climbing was much more dangerous in those days; there were no crampons or other equipment to aid climbers. The group spent hours carving stairs out of the rocks and resting on tiny ledges. The final 600 metres to the summit would involve some very serious climbing.

They were approaching the summit around 5:30 PM when disaster struck. Abbot, who was leading the way, decided to untie himself from the group and climb alone. Fay later commented that, "a moment later, Little, whose attention was for the moment diverted to another portion of the crag, was conscious that something had fallen swiftly past him and I knew only too well what it must have been.

"Thompson and I, standing at the base of the cliff, saw our dear friend falling backwards and headforemost." They "saw him strike the upper margin of the ice slope within 15 feet of [them], turn over completely, and instantly begin rolling down its steep incline."

Abbot died shortly after the group reached him, becoming the first fatality from climbing in North America. Fay and other mountaineers spent the next few months defending all that was special about the man versus mountain experience.

The next year, Swiss climber Peter Sarbach, on the urging of Abbot's family, led a team to the summit of Mount Lefroy, providing the perfect tribute to the fallen climber.

ALBERTA'S CENTENNIAL CITY
BROOKS

Of all the communities to profit in 2005 from Alberta's centennial, perhaps Brooks had the most reason to celebrate. In early January of that year, it opened its new Lakeside Leisure Centre, a state-of-the-art facility that includes wall-sized murals depicting the region's life. And on September 1st, it officially became a city. Not impressive enough, you say? Well, what if I said it became Alberta's Centennial City?

Almost overnight Brooks went from being Alberta's largest town to its current position as Centennial City. Having reached a population of 10,000 in 1996, by the time it was named a city, Brooks had grown by an estimated 3000 people.

No other town in Alberta has that title. No other town will. Brooks will be forever remembered as "the" Centennial City. Quite the nice title to have, don't you think?

MARCO'S RESTAURANT
CALGARY

One of the most popular cocktails was created by bartender Walter Chell, who worked at the Westin Hotel in Calgary. In 1969, to commemorate the opening of Marco's, the hotel's new Italian restaurant, Chell concocted his famous drink.

Using Italian cuisine for inspiration, he mixed hand-mashed clams with tomato juice, vodka, Worcestershire sauce, salt, pepper and a celery stick for garnish. His creation was named after a Roman Emperor and the world was introduced to the "Bloody Caesar."

Chell also helped the Mott's company develop its "clamato" juice. The juice has increased the popularity of the drink so much that 250 million Mott's Clamato Caesars are now consumed every year. I wonder who created "Swamp Water" by mixing multiple fountain pop flavours?

Speaking of Calgary Cuisine...

Every year at Calgary's Buzzard's Cowboy Cuisine, an annual Testicle Festival takes place. Not content with just steaks, chicken and fish, Buzzard's offers up some prairie oysters for several weeks during the summer.

How you like your calves' testicles is a personal choice, I suppose. You can have them in pasta sauce if you'd like, but I'm going to stick to the more traditional steak. I've had haggis before, which was weird, but prairie oysters are just plain nuts!

BIG GARGANTUAN & RIDICULOUSLY OVERSIZED

Bison

Is there a difference between a buffalo and a bison? I'm not exactly sure, but I am sure that Wainwright has erected a statue of a bison in honour of the bison that used to roam the area. From 1908 to 1940, the area was home to Buffalo National Park, a park designed to conserve the endangered animals. During those years, over 48,000 bison called the park home. The herd grew so large at times that annual round-ups were needed to thin it. Some of the animals were shipped around the world, others were slaughtered. The buffalo were removed in 1940, and the park turned over to the Department of National Defence. The park was turned into a training camp for the Canadian military, which, in 1945–46, was used as a prisoner-of-war facility and housed over 1000 German officers. Since then, the camp has undergone many restorations and is one of the primary training areas in Canada.

Standing 3 metres tall and made from fibreglass and concrete, the bison statue welcomes visitors from its pedestal on the south side of Highway 14, 200 kilometres southeast of Edmonton in the middle of town. Thankfully, this bison doesn't roam the streets after dark looking for trouble.

BISON BITS

When Edmonton hosted the International Association of Athletics Federations (IAAF) 2001 World Track and Field Championships, statues of bison lined the highway that was then called Calgary Trail, from the Edmonton International Airport to the city centre. Each bison was decorated to show off the colours and cultures of some of the nations whose athletes were competing in the games. Some of these statues were later defaced in a manic case of neutering. There is no word as to whether or not the "prairie oysters" ended up at a certain annual festival down in Calgary.

The few surviving bison can be seen in all their glory at various spots throughout the city, reminding us all of the wonderful cultural event that enriched the city.

ALBERTA'S READING CAPITAL
CARSTAIRS

Situated along the Edmonton-Calgary corridor, Carstairs no longer needs to live in the shadows of the two largest cities in Alberta. In October 2005, the Calgary Public Library spearheaded the first Great Alberta Reading Challenge. The two-day read-off event took place during National Reading Week and involved any Alberta communities that chose to take part.

For 15 minutes on October 19th and 20th, people were encouraged to read anything they wanted, and then log in and record their names and communities. Individuals could win prizes and the community that got the most participants per capita would take home the title of "Alberta's Reading Capital."

Carstairs was that community. I'm hoping that the participants were reading more than emails, but even if it was just that, good for them for reading. I usually just skim and delete them. Except the ones from my mom, cause that would just be rude.

TOWN GROUCH
EVANSBURG

On the Yellowhead Highway about 100 kilometres west of Edmonton, you'll notice an odd little sign on the left-hand side of the road. The community of Evansburg holds an election every year. They don't vote for a mayor, a new police constable or even a beauty queen; they hold an election to determine the Town Grouch.

The winner is licensed to pester, harass, antagonize, criticize, complain and grumble without fear of retribution for the whole year. I know some pretty grumpy people outside of Evansburg who would win this title hands down, but alas, they are not eligible. Feel free to stop in at the local diner for lunch. Just hope the waitress that day isn't the reigning Town Grouch.

RCMP DOG TRAINING FACILITY
INNISFAIL

Man's best friend has never been better prepared than at the Royal Canadian Mounted Police Dog Training Facility, located in Innisfail. The only canine training facility in Canada, this facility is vital to the success of the RCMP throughout the country. What kind of dog is the RCMP looking for? The dog must be courageous, versatile and strong, and adaptable enough to survive under severe weather conditions. German and Belgian shepherds are two classes of dogs that fit the bill perfectly. Dogs must be in perfect physical condition and are selected when they are between 12 and 18 months old.

Basic training is intense, and only 17 percent of the dogs make it through the 17-week program. The dogs, and their handlers, are put to the test physically and mentally, and when they are done, they play a vital role in keeping Canada safe.

Who wants to be a dog handler? Any member of the RCMP can apply, if they meet certain criteria and show an aptitude towards dogs. Currently, there are over 400 names on the waiting list to be dog handlers, and only 112 dog teams across the country.

But it's not all fame and glory. The job is dangerous, and few bonds are stronger than the one between a handler and his dog. Fortunately, the dogs are retired at seven years old, after which they are free to relax their time away.

PUMPKIN FESTIVAL
SMOKY LAKE

If you ever make it up to Smoky Lake in October, keep a look out for Charlie Brown as he scours the area for the Great Pumpkin. Smoky Lake hosts one of North America's largest pumpkin festivals.

The first Saturday in October is the official date for contestants from BC, Alberta and Saskatchewan to haul their gourds to Smoky Lake for a chance to be the winner. On that one day in October, Smoky Lake's population is five times larger than normal, so popular is the event.

Contestants compete in three categories of gourds (and if you can name three categories before reading the following you are much more intelligent than I am): pumpkins, squashes and watermelons. After the weigh-off, and once all awards have been handed out, an auction is held for people to buy their gourd of choice. Half of the proceeds go to the Smoky Lake Christmas Hamper. So next time you feel like sitting in a field on Halloween, waiting for the Great Pumpkin to appear, think twice. Head to Smoky Lake the first Saturday in October and you may have a better chance at seeing him.

FIRST INDOOR RODEO
STAVLEY

Back in June 1929, the town of Stavley, south of Calgary on Highway 2, used its skating rink for a rodeo—the first indoor rodeo in North America and perhaps the world. It was the brainchild of Harry Streeter, and 2006 marks the 49th year of the event, probably interrupted by the war and the depression over the years.

The community has embraced the rodeo, and volunteers, many of whom have been involved for 35-plus years, handle every aspect to make sure it comes off. Volunteers take tickets, shovel dirt, organize and strip the chutes.

There may be other indoor rodeos now that generate greater fanfare, but Stavely was the first. That is definitely worth a YEE HAW!

Angus Shaw

Early pioneers and traders discovered much of Alberta, and Bonnyville has a monument to honour such men standing in front of its museum. Located about 50 kilometres southeast of Cold Lake and nearly 250 kilometres northeast of Edmonton, Bonnyville takes pride in its multicultural heritage and remembers its roots vividly.

The giant statue of trader Angus Shaw, made entirely of local cedar, stands 7 metres tall. Shaw was a trader with the Hudson's Bay Company in the late 1700s. Known as a good trader who got along well with both his men and the local Native people, Shaw established the first European settlement a little ways east of where Bonnyville is today and called it Anshaw after himself.

The statue's creator, Herman Poulin, also created several other monuments in Alberta. The exact weight of the monument is unknown, but by the looks of it, the beaver up in Beaverlodge could have a nice little time with all that wood.

WACKY AND WEIRD... WITHOUT THE PADDED WALLS

ALBERTA RAT CONTROL PROGRAM
LLOYDMINSTER

In operation since 1950, the Alberta Rat Control Program is an Alberta Agriculture initiative aimed at keeping the province rat free. Patrolling an area some 600 kilometres long and 30 kilometres wide along the eastern border of Alberta, the patrollers keep a lookout for the dreaded Norway rat. The rats still try to invade Alberta, but through a systematic detection and eradication technique, the patrollers manage to keep little furry rodents out.

While the Norway rat is shy, nocturnal and pretty easy going, it does cause substantial damage to farmland and is often regarded as a carrier of disease. Aside from that, rats can cause many more problems. They do not hibernate, so they can wreak havoc all year long. Reproduction starts as early as six to eight weeks old, and rats can have up to 10 litters a year—an awfully big problem if left to multiply. And the rats are hardy little guys, with the ability to survive falls of 8 metres and vertically climb walls for several storeys.

The feats are impressive, but the fact that Alberta has a border patrol to keep out rats is truly amazing. And slightly silly…but in a good way.

CENTRE OF ALBERTA
FREEMAN RIVER

Travel 10 kilometres north of the Freeman River RV Park along Grizzly Trail Highway 33, and you will reach the geographical centre of Alberta. This means that you will be at the equidistant point between the province's north and south boundaries, and the equidistant point between its east and west boundaries.

A short 3-kilometre hike from the information booth off the highway will lead you to a cairn that marks the exact centre point. A number of points of interest along the path make the hike more enjoyable, as well as the terrific scenery.

BIG

GARGANTUAN & RIDICULOUSLY OVERSIZED

A Bean, a Sunflower Seed and an Oil Derrick

In the southeastern corner of Alberta, some 50 kilometres west of Medicine Hat, Bow Island residents have not one, not two, but three giant monuments to take pride in, if pride can be derived from such diverse attractions.

Bow Island is called the "Bean Capital of the West," and as such created Pinto MacBean, their 4.6-metre-tall fibreglass pinto bean mascot that signifies the importance of the dry bean industry to the region. Designed by Jane Osborne of Edmonton and built by Peter Soehn of Kelowna, Pinto was erected in 1992 and stands on the north side of Highway 3, near the visitor information centre.

But the bean wasn't the first monument on scene. The people in Bow Island have had an even taller monument to boast about for many years before Pinto came about. Built for a "tallest sunflower seed" contest in the mid-80s, the 9.2-metre-tall, 1905-kilogram steel sunflower stands in front of the Alberta Sunflower Seed Ltd. plant. Made to withstand winds of up to 110 kilometres per hour, the sunflower was designed by Jager Homes out of Calgary.

And finally, the gas fields around Bow Island have their own monument to symbolize their importance to the area and to serve as an historic marker. While actual dimensions are unknown and hard to track down, Bow Island's oil derrick forms the final piece of a economic stability trifecta that will keep the area, her residents and her economic strengths in people's minds and rearview mirrors for a very long time.

"MILE ZERO"
GRIMSHAW

New York has "Ground Zero," and Grimshaw is "Mile Zero." The Mackenzie Highway leading into the north begins in Grimshaw, hence the name "Mile Zero." This numerical anomaly obviously occurs nowhere else along the highway. Highway 35 connects Alberta's northern communities to Edmonton, and Highway 2 connects the eastern and western parts of the province. Grimshaw sits at this junction, making it a valuable location. Far more valuable than the zero tag would imply.

And Speaking of Highways...

The two main highways that traverse the country from east to west both reach their highest points within the province of Alberta. Highway 1, the Trans-Canada Highway, reaches 1643 metres as it climbs through the Kicking Horse Pass on the Alberta/British Columbia border. The Yellowhead Highway, the Trans-Canada's northern sister, reaches the dizzying height of 1152 metres at the Obed Summit, some 250 kilometres west of Edmonton.

SURVEY MARKERS
LLOYDMINSTER

No visit to Lloydminster is complete, or possible, without a glimpse of the four surveyor markers that divide the town. At 30.5 metres tall, these markers line the border of Alberta and Saskatchewan. Lloydminster is Canada's only border city.

The four markers each represent a different piece of history: oil and gas, agriculture, the Barr Colonists and the Native people. The history behind Lloydminster is as unique as any in the world.

Originally settled in 1903 by the Barr Colonists, about 2600 people from England, the town was named after Reverend Lloyd, who led the colonists. The word "minster" means "mother church."

The newly founded hamlet was part of the Northwest Territories until 1905, when Alberta and Saskatchewan were granted provincial status. A problem arose when the 4th meridian, which ran directly through Lloydminster, was chosen as the new border, effectively splitting the town in half.

For a while, the town operated with two distinct municipal councils, two municipal offices and two fire departments. The towns were amalgamated into a single municipality in 1930 when smart men and women decided that common sense might be a good thing. On January 1, 1958, the Town of Lloydminster officially became the City of Lloydminster, the 10th city in Alberta and Saskatchewan.

And Speaking of Lloydminster...

Because of the lack of technology back when the country was still being mapped out, the actual border of Alberta and Saskatchewan is not where the markers in Lloydminster have it marked. With the advent of Global Positioning System (GPS) technology, a more accurate measurement found that the markers are a little off. The matter means little to the people of Lloydminster.

 **Brian Mulroney Bull Rider**

When the world came to Canada, specifically to Vancouver, for Expo 86, the Alberta Government spent $30,000 to construct a giant mechanical Brahma bull, complete with a lifelike figure of then–Prime Minister Brian Mulroney, and put it on display in the Alberta Pavilion at the exposition. Made of fibreglass, metal and wood, the 4.6-metre-tall structure was auctioned off after the Expo ended, and it was purchased by George McKenzie, who donated it to the museum he helped found. What makes this monument special is that the bull is actually mechanical and can move. The rider has yet to be thrown, however.

The monument now resides in the Brownvale North Peace Agricultural Museum, and it captures Mulroney in full cowboy regalia, cowboy hat triumphantly above his head as he "grabs the bull by the horns." Now citizens of Brownvale, located on Highway 2 southwest of Peace River, can remember Mulroney for something other than the GST he left us.

CHRISSIE'S ANTIQUE BOTTLE COLLECTION
ROCKYFORD

Born in 1911, 10 kilometres south of Rockyford, Chrissie Pederson started collecting bottles in 1976. Since then, she's collected over 1000 bottles and they are on display at "Chrissie's Antique Bottle Collection" on Main Street in Rockyford.

Opened to the public in 1995, the collection features bottles from around the world and of varying sizes. From teeny-tiny to gigantic, and with some Avon bottles thrown in for good measure, Chrissie lovingly collected these bottles over the years, and the town is happy to show this unique look at history.

If you want to find Rockyford, head toward Drumheller on Highway 9, turn south on Highway 21 and look for the signs. Odds are, there won't be any bottles to pick up on the side of the road.

And Speaking of Bottles…

According to the Alberta Bottle Depot Association, more than 500 million bottles and containers were collected in Alberta in 2004. Even at just 10 cents per bottle, that's $50 million back into the hands of Albertans. That's a lot of pocket change, eh?

COSMIC RAY STATION
SULPHUR MOUNTAIN

Perched high atop Sulphur Mountain sits an important piece of history. Back in 1956, the National Research Council of Canada built a geophysical laboratory on top of Sulphur Mountain. Why would they do that, you ask?

Well, it was part of International Geophysical Year (1957–58), and 66 countries took part in several scientific disciplines. The study of cosmic rays was a huge undertaking that year, with 99 stations in operation, including nine in Canada. What makes Sulphur Mountain's Cosmic Ray Station so important was the high altitude of its location. The University of Calgary took over the station in 1960, and it closed in 1978; apparently cosmic rays had become a thing of the past.

Visitors can take a hike or a gondola up Sulphur Mountain in Banff National Park and have a peek at the cabin that bears plaques telling of the history of the unusual site.

WETASKIWIN

What is in a name? To the town of Wetaskiwin, everything.
Back when buffalo roamed the prairies, the Blackfoot and
the Cree peoples were bitter enemies. The Blackfoot lived
on the land south of the Red Deer River and the Cree occupied
the north. The river acted as a natural border for the two tribes.
During the summer, the Blackfoot would follow the buffalo
north and across the river. This angered the Cree, so the two
tribes were always at war.

In about 1867, both tribes had young warrior leaders and were
on the verge of war. The leaders decided to take it upon themselves to scout the enemy territory before the upcoming battle.

They crawled through the brush and stumbled upon each other at the top of a hill.

The two chiefs knew they had to fight, but the Blackfoot chief cast aside his rifle to fight with his hands. Seeing this gesture, the Cree chief discarded his knife and the two went at it, hoping to prove to the Great Manitou, the spirit of the Native people, who the best warrior was.

The hand-to-hand combat lasted nearly an hour with neither man gaining a considerable advantage on his opponent. Relentless, they continued, each struggling against the strength of the other man. Finally, they pulled themselves apart and decided to rest. The Blackfoot chief grabbed his pipe and tobacco and started to smoke. The Cree chief could only watch in agony; his pipe had been broken during the battle.

The Blackfoot chief was taking great pleasure in seeing his enemy suffer as he puffed on his pipe. Then suddenly, he offered his enemy the pipe, and the Cree gladly took a few puffs.

During a deep puff, the Cree chief finally realized what he had done. They had shared the pipe, a sacred sign of friendship and peace. Since they were chiefs of their tribes, the peace they shared must also be shared between the tribes.

Both chiefs returned to their tribes and met with the elder chiefs. Later they returned, shared the peace pipe again and forged the sacred bonds of friendship. The peace has endured, and the hills where the chiefs met became known as *Wetaskiwin Spatinow*, "the hills where peace was made."

BIG
GARGANTUAN & RIDICULOUSLY OVERSIZED

"Twelve Foot" Davis

It is worth travelling nearly 500 kilometres northeast of Edmonton to take in the breathtaking scenery that makes up Peace Country, but there are some sights that will capture the imagine that aren't exactly carved by nature.

Most communities have immortalized someone who has achieved a legendary status in some way or another. In Peace River, citizens chose to honour Henry Fuller "Twelve Foot" Davis. Davis was a prospector who earned his nickname by mining $15,000 worth of gold from a 3.7-metre-wide (that's 12 feet in imperial measurements) plot of land between two other gold claims. He grew to legendary status, and a plaque that accompanies the statue gives us insight into how unique this man was. He loved the valley where he lived, he never locked his door and he was generous. I wonder how many current Peace River residents follow his mould; plenty, I would think.

OLD AND PROUD

FORT DUNVEGAN
DUNVEGAN

Travel south of the Peace River to Fairview and you will come across the Historic Fort Dunvegan and the Saint Charles Mission. The restored fort and the adjacent mission are the oldest buildings in northern Alberta.

Established as a trading post in 1805 by the North West Company, Fort Dunvegan soon became a major trading centre for fur traders. In the 1870s, new buildings popped up to deal with the expanding activities, including a new building for the chief factor, who acted professionally as the representative of another person or entity, in this case the North West Company. The structure still stands, albeit refurbished, and it is located just west of the bridge. The Mission and adjoining Rectory were built in the 1880s and still stand on their original spots on the east side of the bridge. The two buildings are a major feature of the Fort Dunvegan Historic Site.

The site became a provincial park in 1992 and incorporated a "barrier-free" campground soon after. The visitor centre arrived in 1994, and visitors have been flocking to the site ever since.

BIG

GARGANTUAN & RIDICULOUSLY OVERSIZED

Ice Cream Sundae

One year less one week to the day the 1987 tornado ripped through Edmonton, Palm Dairies, under the supervision of Mike Rogiani, gave the people of Edmonton something to cheer about. They created the world's largest ice cream sundae.

With over 20 tonnes of ice cream, 4 tonnes of syrup and over 237 kilograms of toppings, this giant dessert could have been shared by all. I don't remember having any of it, which upsets me, actually. You can't beat a sundae on a warm July day, unless you don't like sundaes, and then you can't beat whatever it is you like better.

ALBERTA'S OLDEST COMMUNITY
FORT CHIPEWYAN

At over 200 years old, Fort Chip, as it is know to those who like to keep things informal, is Alberta's oldest community. Accessible only by air, this tiny hamlet some 225 air kilometres north of Fort McMurray stands on the border of Wood Buffalo National Park. What does the location mean? Well, Fort Chip's nearest neighbour is the largest free-roaming herd of buffalo in the world. No word on whether or not they like to crash house parties, but I'm betting their wings are good.

FORT EDMONTON PARK
EDMONTON

This park, surrounded by modern-day Edmonton, is Canada's largest historical park. Actually, Fort Edmonton Park is four living history museums in one handy location. Talk about a good value for your entertainment dollar.

Starting at the refurbished Fort Edmonton itself, visitors are taken back to 1846 and can see the way things looked when the Hudson's Bay Company was running the show. With costumed interpreters providing insight, visitors can even take part in some of their daily duties.

A quick trip up 1885 Street starts the tour of the second historic park. Travel by stagecoach for the best views of what Edmonton was like when only 385 people called her home. Next up is 1905 Street, set in the capital city of the recently appointed province. Here's your chance to take advantage of the new invention called the telephone. Sorry, emails are not available. From 1905, journey over to 1920 Street where you can have fun playing mini-golf, which was all the rage back then. Hop on a street car and return to the parking lot to return to modern times. All in all, the country's largest historical park is sure to amaze and delight.

FORT WHOOP-UP
LETHBRIDGE

This site, located in Lethbridge, is the perfect place to relive Alberta's Wild West ways. The original Fort Whoop-Up was built in 1869 by Montana businessmen. The Fort soon became renowned as the most notorious whiskey trading post in Alberta. The Blackfoot would bring their buffalo pelts and trade them for whiskey and guns.

The fort features furnished rooms with trade goods, audio-visual presentations, wagon rides and daily historic vignettes. It interprets the period between 1865 and 1892, when the last bull train made the trip from Fort Benton, Montana.

SQUEAKY THE MOUSE
IRRICANA

The little town of Irricana goes to great lengths to make itself stand out from the rest of Alberta's communities. It nearly warranted mention with the weirdest Alberta sites, but fell just a little short.

No visit to Irricana is complete without a sighting of Squeaky, a mouse who serves as the town mascot. Squeaky goes out and about, bringing joy to many of the town's events. Believe me when I say that Squeaky is not a mouse to be afraid of.

The town also has five murals located on the walls of various buildings. Members of the community helped design and create the murals, and if you look closely enough, you may see a single country mouse incorporated into every single mural. I'm still looking, so don't ask me for help.

BIG

GARGANTUAN & RIDICULOUSLY OVERSIZED

Cream Can and Wheat

Take a cream can and wheat stalks and what do you get? Cream of Wheat? No, you get a moving homage to the pioneers that founded a region with little more than hard work and togetherness.

Markerville, which is located on Highway 54 west of Innisfail, is the proud home of the Cream Can and Wheat monument. With its bevelled top, two open handles near the neck, and shiny surface, the monument really stands out.

The total height of the silver cream can is 4.6 metres, but what it represents to the area, which owes so much to the creamery and grain farming, is far from measurable. The plaque on the monument even includes some words from famous Icelandic poet turned Alberta resident Stephan G. Stephansson:

1888–1988 Dedicated to the pioneers of Markerville and District who prepared the way. They did so much with so little. The best that was in me forever shall live. The sun over darkness prevails.

OLD SMOKEY
IRRICANA

Outside the Irricana Hotel stands the statue of a horse. Local resident Mel Brown (who also has a trail named after him—one that links the west end of Founders Park to the Pioneer Acres Museum Site just north of Irricana), was often seen riding his favourite horse "Old Smokey" along the railroad tracks. When Brown died, he had no family to leave his money to so he commissioned the statue as a memorial to himself. Seeing as though he spent a lot of his time at the hotel, it was a logical spot for the statue.

POLICE OUTPOST
PROVINCIAL PARK

I must admit, I had never heard of this park before. Now I plan to visit. Located on a small lake on the United States border, this is Alberta's southernmost provincial park.

A North-West Mounted Police post was established here in 1891, and it served to protect the 48 residents from whiskey and gun runners. The post closed within a few years, after the need to protect the few residents dwindled due to a lack of whiskey running.

At just 223 hectares, it is a small park, but it is gaining a large reputation with boaters, fishers and hikers for its quality scenery and wildlife.

HELL'S HALF ACRE
TURNER VALLEY

We should all raise a glass and thank Turner Valley for starting the oil boom that has led to unprecedented wealth in Alberta. The first well sprung up in 1914 and offered some hope, but in 1924, the mother lode was discovered and really put Turner Valley on the map.

The oil from those wells was so pure it could be used in automobiles straight from the well, and the Turner Valley area became the cornerstone of Alberta's oil industry. For a period of 30 years, the region was the top oil producer in the British Empire.

Even when the oil was piped into Calgary, there still remained more than was needed. Excess oil was piped from the plant and discharged into a ravine, where it was burned. During the Depression, when workers from across Canada and the U.S. would come to Turner Valley looking for work in the winter, they would huddle on the banks of the ravine where the oil was burning to keep warm. Rather fittingly, the area was known as Hell's Half Acre.

Grain Elevator Sundial

Remember that scene in the first *Crocodile Dundee* movie in which Mick Dundee secretly looks at Wally's watch then stares at the sun and predicts the time? He wouldn't have had to bother if he visited Sangudo and its Sundial-Elevator. Of course, Mick Dundee was in Australia and not in the village of Sangudo, almost 200 kilometres northwest of Edmonton on Highway 43.

The only known sundial built in the shape of one of the country grain elevators that used to dot the prairies, it is also one of the biggest sundials, with a height of over 6.4 metres and a total weight of over 40 tonnes, including the marker stones. So unique is this sundial, the village of Sangudo has copywritten its design.

The sundial acts as a tourist attraction, village landmark and geographical marker, a village logo, village entrance sign, and as entrance beautification. The slope of the roof is 54° 54', which corresponds to the north latitude of Sangudo and enables it to work as a simple sundial. Certain types of sundials, this one included, must be made specific to the location of intended use and as such will only tell local solar time. Sangudo Solar Time, on average, is 40 minutes behind Mountain Standard Time. The sundial's unique design and ability to tell a time only available in Sangudo makes it the only one of its kind in the world.

My Community is Weirder Than Yours!

*Some communities need more than just a blurb
to describe how unique or special they are.
What separates these communities from others in the
province is the great lengths at which they go to be just
plain unusual. Have a look for yourself. I might be biased,
but I think these arc definitely the big hitters
when it comes to weird Alberta places.*

DRUMHELLER
DINOSAURS

Where to begin with Drumheller? How about we start with the dinosaurs—and not the ones they dig up in this fossil-rich region.

At one time, nearly 30 dinosaurs were built in an area called Prehistoric Park. The park closed nearly a decade ago, and now the dinosaur statues occupy spots around town. Most are quiet, keep to themselves, like a morning coffee or two to kickstart the day. Some may feel the need to roar once and while, but this hasn't been confirmed. Also in the park was a 9.2-metre-high statue of Jesus that remains on the hill where it was originally placed.

Drumheller is also home to the largest dinosaur in the world, a massive Tyrannosaurus Rex that stands over 26 metres tall and 46 metres long. Dino 2000, as he's called, actually offers a viewing area from inside the dinosaur's mouth. A series of 62 stairs start at the tail and climb inside the beast's belly, opening up into an observation platform that can hold about 8 to 12 people. Fossils and bones are embedded in the walls of the enclosed staircase to impress photo-hungry tourists. Interestingly enough, a real Tyrannosaurus only stood about 4.8 metres high.

We love the fake dinosaurs, but what about the real ones they're finding? Or should I say pieces of real ones they're finding. The Royal Tyrrell Museum of Paleontology is a world-class facility dedicated to showcasing fossils, from the tiniest to the largest. As Canada's only institution devoted to paleontology, the Royal Tyrrell Museum is certainly one-of-a-kind.

Opened in 1985, the museum houses an astonishing 110 million specimens in its collection. Dinosaur Hall, the most popular of the exhibits, features 40 full dinosaur skeletons mounted for perfect photographing opportunities. Here you'll see the Tyrannosaur and the mighty Albertosaurus, found in the region by Joseph B. Tyrrell.

HOMESTEAD ANTIQUE MUSEUM

If you're looking for a piece of early Canadiana, then the Homestead Antique Museum is the place for you. Located just a short drive from the Royal Tyrrell Museum, this museum offers a hard-to-duplicate assortment of Canadiana with thousands of items on display.

With items ranging from Indian artifacts and pioneer ranching tools to antique toys and musical instruments, this is a site to behold. Old cars, tractors and a steam engine can be seen, and there is even a beauty parlour and barbershop on display.

THE LITTLE CHURCH

The Drumheller region has 11 places to worship but none more popular than the Little Church. This tiny church is visited by 10,000 people a year, but only six can go inside at a time because the building measures a mere 2.1 x 3.4 metres. Located on the Dinosaur Trail, it is easily accessible and well worth a visit.

BIG
GARGANTUAN &
RIDICULOUSLY
OVERSIZED

Squirt the Skunk

What has painted toenails, a giant smiling face, stands in a campground while holding flowers and was created thanks to a contest for a new town mascot? Squirt the Skunk, of course. He's Beiseker's new mascot. Though most campers would run in fear at the sight of a skunk in their campground, Squirt stands, tail curled towards its head, welcoming visitors to the small town west of Drumheller and north of Calgary. Squirt was created by Peter Soehn of Kelowna, an artist responsible for several other Alberta monuments. Squirt, pedestal included, stands nearly 4 metres tall and is made from fibreglass, resilient enough for all the weather Alberta can summon.

Built in 1992 with funding from the Alberta government, Squirt was dreamed up when the town held a contest to find a mascot. But why would a town decide that a skunk would be the ideal mascot to capture the image of a friendly community? Because Squirt the skunk is a symbol of the fact that it "makes scents to stop in Beiseker." A cuter skunk I challenge you to find.

ST. PAUL
UFO LANDING PAD

If they are out there, and I'm talking about aliens, the good people of St. Paul will be waiting for them. And they've given them a place to land as well. St. Paul, Alberta is home to the world's first UFO landing pad. Weird? Very. Interesting? Extremely.

Back in the mid 1960s, the Canadian government encouraged communities to build centennial monuments. St. Paul had originally won prestige for completing its first monument in 1964, the St. Paul Recreation Centre. It was the first Centennial Project completed in Canada. But it wasn't going to stop there. No park, no statue, no museum would suffice; it had to be something to capture the imagination of the nation.

The idea for a UFO landing pad actually came from W.R. Treleaven of Hamilton, Ontario and Ken Reed of Calgary. Promotion of the project was assumed by the St. Paul Centennial Committee.

A time capsule was sealed into the backstop of the 130-tonne concrete landing pad, set to be opened in 2067. Inside the time capsule are letters from then-mayor Ernest Manning and the president of the St. Paul Chamber of Commerce.

The landing pad was built on land donated for the project and broken by the Honourable Grant MacEwan, lieutenant-governor of Alberta in 1967. Joining people from the town for the occasion was the Minister of National Defence. The Honourable Paul Hellyer arrived via helicopter.

The total cost was a paltry $11,000, since many of the materials and tools were donated by local companies. In the 1990s, the Tourist Information Centre was constructed along with an interpretive UFO display, which includes alleged photos of UFOs, crop circles and other unexplained phenomena. Naturally, the information centre is shaped like a UFO.

Visitors have come from all over the world (and only this world so far), and in 2000 the site hosted an International UFO conference. Notable visitors to the sight include Queen Elizabeth II and Mother Theresa.

And Speaking of UFOs…

In 2001, Canadian sightings of UFOs rose 42 percent over numbers in 2000. Albertans witnessed 40 UFOs during the year, the third highest provincial rate in the country, behind BC and Ontario.

BIG
GARGANTUAN &
RIDICULOUSLY
OVERSIZED

Peter Fiddler

Much of Alberta was discovered by fur traders working for the Hudson's Bay Company, and Elk Point was no different. Legend has it that fur trader Peter Fiddler's canoe sprung a leak and, like the native people had done before him, he grabbed some gumbo mud from the river bank and plugged the hole. The mud contained oil, which oozed up from the ground. To honour Fiddler, a 9.8-metre-tall statue was carved by Herman Poulin and his trusty chainsaw, and it stands on the west side of Highway 41 in Elk Point, about 250 kilometres east of Edmonton. No pictures or photos of Fiddler were available, so townsperson Bill Doty posed for the statue design. Constructed in 1992 as part of Elk Point's bicentennial project, the carving is one of a few interesting sights within the town's limits.

TORRINGTON
GOPHER HOLE MUSEUM

What Torrington has to offer Alberta in the weird department is nothing short of unusual. Not content with being another small Alberta town, Torrington decided to really put its name on the map.

The farmers in Torrington, north and east of Calgary, have long been pestered by gophers. The gopher problem is so bad that the little curious rodents (have you ever been driving down a country road and seen one stand up to get a closer look at you speeding car?) have to be killed. But sometimes, there can be beauty in death.

The "World Famous Gopher Hole Museum" has around 50 dead, stuffed gophers in 31 delightful dioramas, each depicting a scene from Torrington life. Can't visualize what a Mountie would look like with whiskers and paws? Thanks to Mountie Gopher, now you can. The museum features gophers in a beauty parlour, gophers playing pool, a gopher working as a blacksmith and even the Reverend Gopher standing at his pulpit.

The museum receives a great amount of positive feedback from thousands of visitors each year. However, the good people at PETA (People for the Ethical Treatment of Animals) have had problems with the museum. When the museum opened in 1996, the furor that PETA created generated what amounted to thousands of dollars worth of free publicity, and ultimately led people to the museum so they could check it out for themselves.

The Gopher Hole Museum has put the town on the map, and Torrington has embraced the gopher as its symbolic critter. Clem T. Gofur greets visitors driving into town from the east on Highway 27. The 3.7-metre-tall, overalled, cowboy hat-wearing, smiling varmint has graced Torrington since 1991. As the official town mascot, Clem probably likes the museum and is glad to see his little buddies proudly on display. And if you look closely as you drive through town, you'll notice that all the fire hydrants are painted to look like Clem's offspring. In India, the cow is sacred; could the gopher be far behind in Torrington?

And Speaking of Taxidermy…

At the Fuchs Wildlife exhibit at the Barr Colony Heritage Cultural Centre in Lloydminster, it is believed that visitors can view North America's largest display of one person's taxidermy. The display features mounted birds and smaller mammals.

VULCAN
SPACE SHIP INFORMATION CENTRE

Where to begin with what is probably Alberta's weirdest community? And I mean that nicely. Vulcan is so unique that it makes me beam. Kind of like "Beam me up, Scotty," but that would be too obvious.

Vulcan was around long before the television series *Star Trek* hit the airwaves in the 1960s. Captain Kirk and the beloved Mr. Spock quickly became pop culture icons, but none more so than the calm and always logical Vulcan. His pointed ears made him stand out from the other members of the starship, as did his Vulcan past. As the popularity of the show grew, the town of Vulcan was quick to jump on the Trek bandwagon.

How many people have received information from a spaceship-shaped information centre? If you travel to Vulcan, Alberta you will. Opened in 1998, the Vulcan Tourism and Trek Station has plenty of information about the surrounding areas for tourists, and plenty of nostalgia for Trekkies.

Life-sized cardboard pictures of *Star Trek* characters are on hand to "pose" for photos with diehard fans or anyone with a sense of humour. The Klingon landscape backdrop takes people away from Earth and deposits them on a different landscape for extra-special photos.

Check your email in the Cyber Station or perhaps send a Vulcan postcard online to your friends around the world—or galaxy, I suppose. Naturally, the good-natured citizens of Vulcan have plenty of entertaining displays for small human folk, and souvenirs abound. *Star Trek* memorabilia is always popular, but not surprisingly, the plastic Vulcan ears are the big seller—over 30,000 sets so far.

What would a town like Vulcan be without a giant Starship Enterprise? Unveiled on June 10th, 1995, the Enterprise was based on the original starship from the first television series. Located at the main entrance to town, it immediately implies that Vulcan embraces its commonality with pop culture.

At 9.4 metres long and 2.7 metres deep, the starship weighs 5 tonnes and is mounted on a concrete base to keep it sturdy. Illuminated at night for a futuristic effect, the starship would not look out of place on a Hollywood movie set.

Why go through all the trouble of building a space station information centre and a Starship *Enterprise* and selling Vulcan ears if you aren't going to have a festival to celebrate them? In June, Vulcan holds Galaxyfest and Spockdays. The events have been amalgamated and are sure to bring Klingons, Vulcans, Romulans, Borgs and even humans out for the festival. With guest appearances by actors who have appeared on the various incarnations of *Star Trek* over the years, the event is a must attend for any true Trekkie. All in all, Vulcan is "boldly going where no Alberta community has gone before."

ABOUT THE AUTHOR

Geraint Isitt

Geraint Isitt lives in Alberta's capital but isn't sure which of Alberta's cities he likes the best. He came to the province with his family in 1975 and has called Alberta home ever since. His sense of adventure and fun has taken him all over Alberta and around the world. He travels to the UK as often he can to visit his relatives there, but he still feels most at home in Edmonton. When he's not writing, Geraint can be found on the soccer field or the golf course or just relaxing with his friends. He chose writing as a career after his elementary school teacher told him he would be a great storyteller because he talked in class so much. Geraint is a graduate of Grant MacEwan's Professional Writing degree program and currently works as a technical writer and, of course, is working on the great Canadian novel.

ABOUT THE ILLUSTRATORS

Graham Johnson

Graham Johnson is an Edmonton-based illustrator and graphic designer. When he isn't drawing or designing, he...well...he's always drawing or designing! On the off-chance you catch him not doing one of those things, he's probably cooking, playing tennis or poring over other illustrations.

Roger Garcia

Roger Garcia immigrated to Canada from El Salvador at the age of seven. Because of the language barrier, he had to find a way to communicate with other kids. That's when he discovered the art of tracing. It wasn't long before he mastered this highly skilled technique, and by age 14, he was drawing weekly cartoons for the *Edmonton Examiner*. He taught himself to paint and sculpt; then in high school and college, Roger skipped class to hide in the art room all day in order to further explore his talent. Currently, Roger's work can be seen in a local weekly newspaper and in places around Edmonton.

NOW ENJOY THESE FUN- AND FACT-FILLED BOOKS OF ALBERTA AND CANADIAN TRIVIA...

Bathroom Book of Alberta History

Alberta celebrated its centennial in 2005, so the province's history technically is a short one. However, the populated history of the region spans many centuries, starting with First Nations tribes that travelled the area 8000 years ago in pursuit of massive herds of bison. Europeans first reached the province in the mid-18th century, when fur trader Anthony Henday came calling on the Blackfoot. The Mounties got their start 100 years or so later when they were sent to Alberta to shut down U.S. whiskey traders. This highly entertaining book features these and hundreds of other interesting facts about Alberta's past.

$9.95 • ISBN10: 1-897278-17-9 • ISBN13: 978-1-897278-17-8 • 5.25" X 8.25" • 168 pages

Bathroom Book of Alberta Trivia

This book is bound to entertain with hundreds of oddball facts about Alberta past and present. Which Alberta city holds the world record for eating the largest ice cream sundae? Which famous television actor was born in Edmonton? How did Dead Man Flats get its name? Find out the answers to these and a multitude of other completely trivial questions with the *Bathroom Book of Alberta Trivia*.

$9.95 • ISBN10: 0-9739116-2-X • ISBN13: 978-0-9739116-2-6 • 5.25" X 8.25" • 168 pages

Bathroom Book of Canadian Trivia

An entertaining and lighthearted collection of illustrated factoids from across the country. You'll find beasties from the elusive lake monster Ogopogo to Canada's national emblem, the beaver—and you'll find culture and crime, such as the Calgary Stampede or the number of cars stolen in Canada and where they were stolen. This book has a myriad of informative tidbits to satisfy your curiosity and tickle your funny bone.

$9.95 • ISBN10: 0-9739116-0-3 • ISBN13: 978-0-9739116-0-2 • 5.25" X 8.25" • 144 pages

Bathroom Book of Canadian History

From wild weather to odd prime ministers, Canada's amazing history is full of the comic, the tragic and the just plain weird. You'll enjoy this fun collection of fascinating facts about our illustrious and often peculiar past.

$9.95 • ISBN10: 0-9739116-1-1 • ISBN13: 978-0-9739116-1-9 • 5.25" X 8.25" • 144 pages

Weird Canadian Places

The Canadian landscape is home to some pretty odd sights; for example, the UFO landing pad in St. Paul, Alberta, the ice hotel in Québec City or Casa Loma, Canada's only castle. This book humorously inventories many real estate oddities found across the country. Welcome to the True North—strange to see.

$9.95 • ISBN10: 0-9739116-4-6 • ISBN13: 978-0-9739116-4-0 • 5.25" X 8.25" • 168 pages

Available from your local bookseller or by contacting the distributor, Lone Pine Publishing, at 1-800-661-9017.

www.lonepinepublishing.com